A Survey of the Scriptures

by the
Rev. Johnny Calvin Smith, M.A.B.S.

Pastor of
Mount Moriah
Missionary Baptist Church
Dallas, Texas

Searchlight Press
Dallas, Texas

A Survey of the Scriptures

ISBN#: 978-1-936497-20-1

Scripture taken from the
Authorized "King James" Version
of the English Bible

Searchlight Press
Who are you looking for?
Publishers of thoughtful Christian books since 1994.
5634 Ledgestone Drive
Dallas, TX 75214-2026
214-662-5494
info@Searchlight-Press.com
www.Searchlight-Press.com

Manufactured in the United States of America

Dedication

It is with a great degree of gratitude to the Lord for enabling me to compile this book. This study grows out of the enlightenment from various instructors of Southern Bible Institute and Dallas Theological Seminary who have enriched my life with so much knowledge from the word of God. I would like to thank my beautiful wife, Violet Smith. She has been invaluable to me and a great source of strength to me as this book was being complied. Special thanks also go to my wonderful children: Joy D. McBeth (Brad), Jonathan C. Smith (Christina), and Jared R. Smith. My children have been tremendous in encouraging me to remain steadfast in the study of God's word. In addition, I want to thank God for my grandchildren, children so endearing to my heart: Josiah, Jillian, Jeremiah, Jessica, and Jackson. Finally, I would like to thank my church family, the Mount Moriah Missionary Baptist Church of Dallas, for allowing me to share my passion in preaching and teaching God's inerrant word.

Rev. Johnny C. Smith

Table of Contents

Notes

The Old Testament

An Outline of the Old Testament

The Periods of Bible History

I. Genesis Chapters 1-11, Creation to Abraham (from creation to 2000 B.C.)
Prominent Features of this Period
        A. Creation – Chapter 1
        B. Creation of Man – Chapter 2
        C. Fall of Man – Chapter 3
        D. Murder of Abel by Cain – Chapter 4
        E. Flood – Chapters 6-9
        F. Tower of Babel – Chapter 11
        G. Call of Abraham – Chapter 11

II. Genesis Chapters 12-50, Book of Job. Abraham to Moses (2000 B.C. – 1500 B.C.)
Prominent Persons of this Period are: Abraham, Isaac, Jacob, and Joseph
        A. The Call and Experiences of Abraham – Chapters 12-25
        B. The Career of Isaac and His Experiences – Chapters 25-26
        C. The Career of Jacob and His Experiences – Chapters 27-36
        D. The Career and Triumph of Joseph – Chapters 37-50
        E. The events of the book of Job occur during

the patriarchal period. Charles C. Ryrie, Ryrie Study Bible, Moody Press Chicago, 1994, p. 788.

III. Exodus, Leviticus, Numbers, Deuteronomy. The Exodus (1500 B.C. – 1460 B.C.) This period is covered in the books of Exodus – Deuteronomy.

    A. The book of Genesis closes mentioning the death of Joseph. Joseph dies being 110.

    B. Moses is raised up as Israel's leader and under his leadership the children of Israel depart from Egypt.

    C. After their departure from Egypt, they spend one year at Mt. Sinai and receive the law.

    D. They wander in the wilderness for nearly 40 years because of disobedience.

    E. Moses dies being 120 years old and Joshua succeeds him.

IV. Joshua. The Conquest of Canaan (1460 B.C. – 1450 B.C.)

    A. Joshua leads across the Jordan, conquering Jericho and Ai and achieving other military victories.

    B. After the inhabitants of the land are reduced, the land is divided among the 12 tribes.

C. Joshua dies being 110 years old.

V. Judges, Ruth. The Judges (1450 B.C. – 1100 B.C.)-The record is found in the books Judges and Ruth.
    A. There are 15 Judges.
    B. This period is marked by apostasy, decline and failure.
    C. The Last and greatest of the Judges is Samuel.

VI. I & II Samuel, I & II Kings, I & II Chronicles, Psalms, Proverbs, Ecclesiastes, Song of Solomon, Isaiah, Jerermiah, Lamentations, Ezekiel, Daniel, Hosea, Joel, Amos, Obadiah, Jonah, Micah, Nahum, Habakkak, Zephaniah, The Kingdom (1100 B.C. – 586 B.C.) This period is recorded in I&II Samuel, I&II Kings, and I&II Chronicles
    A. Israel demands a king, and Samuel anoints Saul, and he reigns for 40 years.
    B. David succeeds Saul and he reigns for 40 years.
    C. Solomon succeeds David and he reigns for 40 years.
    D. After the death of Solomon, the kingdom is split, with Jeroboam being the first king of Israel, and Rehoboam being the first king of Judah. There are 19 wicked kings for the

Northern kingdom and 19 kings and one queen for the Southern kingdom.

E.   The Northern kingdom falls to the Assyrian Empire in 722 B.C.

F.   The Southern kingdom falls to the Babylonian Empire in 586 B.C Note: There are three deportations of Judah to Babylon. They are: 605 B.C., 597 B.C., and 586 B.C.

G.   Psalms to Song of Solomon are recorded during this period.

H.   The prophets from Isaiah to Zephaniah speak during this period.

VII.   Ezra, Nehemiah, Esther, Haggai, Zechariah, Malachi. The Restoration (538 B.C – 391 B.C)-The records of this period are found in the books of Ezra, Nehemiah, and Esther.

A. In 538 B.C, Cyrus issues a decree allowing the Jews to return to Jerusalem.

B.   The leaders during this period are Ezra, Nehemiah, and Zerubbabel.

C. The Temple's foundation is started in 536 B.C.

D. The Temple is completed in 516 B.C.

E.   The prophets from Haggai to Malachi speak during this period.

VIII. Between the Testaments (391 B.C. – 5 B.C.)

A. The Old Testament closes with the Persians in control.

B. The Old Testament is translated from Hebrew to Greek, called the "Septuagint" under the reign of Alexander the Great's successors.

C. The Jews pass through many experiences under the dominion of the Greeks and Romans.

God is unfolding His plan for the arrival of Christ, the only Savior for man ~ Galatians 4:4

SEVEN DISPENSATIONS

A dispensation is a period of time in which God deals with man in a certain way in order to prove to man that he cannot be righteous without God. A dispensation can be defined as a stage in the progressive revelation of God, constituting a distinctive stewardship or rule of life. The recognition of the dispensations sheds more light on the whole message of the Bible than any other aspect of biblical study. Each dispensation begins with a governmental test and ends with God's judgment.

1. The Dispensation of Innocence Ref: Genesis 1:26 – 3:6.
2. The Dispensation of Conscience Ref: Genesis 3:7-8:19
3. The Dispensation of Human Government Ref: Genesis 8:20-11:9
4. The Dispensation of Promise Ref: Genesis 11:10 – Exodus 19:2
5. The Dispensation of Law Ref: Exodus 19:3 – Acts 1
6. The Dispensation of Grace Ref: Acts 2 – Rapture of the church
7. The Dispensation of The Kingdom Ref: Isaiah 2:1-4; 11, Matthew 24, Revelation 19, 20

1 Lewis Sperry Chafer, Major Bible Themes, Zondervan Publishing House, Grand Rapids, Michigan, 1974, pp. 126.

Dispensationalism

Dispensationalism finds in God's word evidence of a series of dispensations or "economies" under which He manages the world. These dispensations are successive stages in God's revelation of His purpose. They do not entail different means of salvation, for the means of salvation is the same in - all periods of time. - By grace through faith we are saved. (Ephesians 2:10). There is some disagreement as to the number of dispensations, the most common number being seven. Thus man is first in the dispensation of innocence. Then comes conscience, human government, promise, law, and grace. The seventh, kingdom, is yet to come. Many dispensationalists emphasize that recognizing the dispensational period of a given scripture is crucial.

Dispensationalists also stress the distinction between Israel and the church. The promises made to Israel are applied to Israel and not to the church. The church and Israel are two separate entities. God interrupts His special dealings with Israel and will resume them after the church age. We must not confuse the two divine Kingdoms in scripture. The Kingdom of heaven is Jewish, Davidic and Messianic. When it is rejected by national Israel during Jesus' ministry, its appearance on earth is postponed. The Kingdom of

God, on the other hand, is more inclusive. It encompasses all moral intelligences obedient to the will of God - the angels and the saints from every period of time.

Through obedience to the gospel's call, we become members of the church, the ecclesia, the "called out ones." During this parenthesis in God's economy, God grafts a distinct group called the "church." God will indeed resume His dealing with the rejected nation of Israel, only after the church is" "caught up" or raptured out of this world.

Revelation 3:10 says "Because thou hast kept the word of my patience, I also will keep thee from the hour of temptation, which shall come upon all the world, to try them that dwell upon the earth."

Israel's Judges

First Group leaders (1300-1155 B. C.)
Othniel
Ehud
Shamgar
Deborah (with Barak)

Second Group leaders (1148 – 1105 B.C.)
Gideon
Abimelech
Tola
Jair

Third Group leaders (1105 – 1099 B. C.)
Jephthah
Ibzan
Elon
Abdon

Fourth Group leaders (1085 – 1065 B. C.)
Samson
Eli
Samuel

Israel's Kings

United Kingdom
Saul
1051 – 1011 BC
David
1011 – 971 BC
Solomon
971 – 931 BC

Divided Kingdom
(931-586 B.C.)

Southern Kingdom	Northern Kingdom
Judah 931-586 BC	Israel 931-722 BC
Rehoboam 931-913 BC	Jeroboam I 931-910 B
Abijah 913-911 BC	Nadab 910-909 BC
Asa 911-870 BC	Baasha 909-886 BC
Jehoshaphat 873-848 BC	Elah 886-885 BC

Southern Kingdom	Northern Kingdom
Jehoram 848-841 BC	Zimri 885 BC
Ahaziah 841 BC	Omri 885-874 BC
Athaliah (Queen) 841-835 BC	Ahab 874-853 BC
Joash 835-796 BC	Ahaziah 853-852 BC
Amaziah 796-767 BC	Jehoram 852-841 BC
Uzziah 790-739 BC	Jehu 841-814 BC
Jotham 750-731 BC	Jehoahaz 814-798 BC
Ahaz 731-715 BC	Jehoash 798-782 BC
Hezekiah 715-686 BC	Jeroboam II 782-753 BC
Manasseh 695-642 BC	Zechariah 753 BC

Southern Kingdom	Northern Kingdom
Amon 642-640 BC	Shallum 752 BC
Josiah 640-609 BC	Menahem 752-742 BC
Jehoahaz 609 BC	Pekahiah 742-740 BC
Jehoiakim 609-597 BC	Pekah 740-732 BC
Jehoiachin 597 BC	Hoshea 732-722 BC
Zedekiah 597-586BC	Fall of Samaria (722 BC)
Fall of Jerusalem (586 BC)	

Source: <u>Ryrie Study Bible</u>, Charles Caldwell Ryrie, Th. D, Ph. D., Moody Publishers, Chicago, 1994

Genesis

The word "Genesis" means beginning, origin, or source. The book of Genesis provides the basis for the understanding of the rest of the bible. Who is the author? It is commonly accepted that Moses is the human author. The book provides or gives an account of the beginning of everything except God, such as the beginning of creation, the beginning of man, the beginning of sin, death, family, civilization, government and nations.

The first eleven chapters of Genesis provide a history of mankind in general in which the geographical setting begins in Eden and culminates in Haran (Genesis 1-11). In this section, God is dealing with mankind in general. After He creates Adam and places him in a perfect environment, Adam sins. God intervenes in marvelous love and provides a sufficient covering for Adam and Eve (Genesis 3:21). Since the entrance of sin in the human race, civilization becomes even more wicked, with God destroying the whole civilization with the exception of eight souls, Noah and his posterity.

Beginning in Genesis chapter 12, God begins to deal with a distinct race of people, the Hebrews. He promises them a land, seed, and that they will be blessed. In other words, through Abraham all of the nations of the world will be blessed. Abraham is noted in the bible as a man of unusual faith. One passage in Genesis really brings out the fact that Abraham possessed unusual faith in God, for Genesis 15:6 says: "And he (Abraham) believed in the Lord; and He (God) counted it to him (Abraham) for righteousness."

If Abraham is to have a great nation, then he must have children. How could he be great and have a great posterity if he didn't have children? God is equal to that great dilemma by providing Abraham a son named Isaac, even when Abraham was one hundred and Sarai was ninety. From Genesis chapters 12-50, we have the history of the great patriarchs: Abraham, Isaac, and Jacob.

God blesses Abraham's son, Isaac to have children, namely, Esau and Jacob. In God's sovereign way, He chooses Jacob, with Jacob having a great family of twelve sons (called the nation of Israel), and one daughter, Dinah. One of Jacob's sons, Joseph, occupies the remaining chapters 37-50. Joseph, who is the object of his father's love, becomes also the object of his brothers' hatred. Through an act of cruelty, his brethren cast him into a pit and he is sold to the Ishmaelites for twenty pieces of silver and deported to Egypt. God blesses him and he becomes second in command to Potiphar.

Meanwhile, a famine occurs in the land of Canaan and Joseph's brethren come to Egypt seeking food. In God's providential way, Joseph becomes the means of help for his brethren. The whole family comes to Egypt and they are given the land of Goshen. Jacob dies and his brethren become anxious in thinking that Joseph will now seek revenge for what they did to him. However, Joseph disquiets them by saying: "But as for you, ye thought evil against me, but God meant it unto good, to bring to pass, as it is this day, to save much people alive" (Genesis 50: 20).

Exodus

Exodus gives an account of God's people as they sojourn in the land of Egypt. While there, they become an enslaved people, actually being in that condition for four hundred and thirty years, rounded to four hundred years. Although in that predicament, God never abandons them, just as He never abandons His children on this side of the rapture.

In this book, we have an account of Israel's infancy as a nation. This small family of seventy increases to a mighty nation, multiplying to nearly two to three million strong as they exited Egypt (Exodus12:37). The word Exodus can mean "to exit," "to depart" or "to go out." Many critics attempt to discredit Moses as the author, but their arguments are weak and carry no merit at all. It is commonly accepted that this book records the forty-year wilderness walk of Israel, from 1445 B.C. to 1405 B.C. led by Moses. The testimony of others will confirm his authorship (St. John 1:45, Romans 10:5, Mark 7:10, Luke 20:37, St. John 5:46-47).

The book carries a dual theme of redemption and deliverance. As one reads the book, it is apparent that the key word is redemption (Exodus 6:6). Redemption is taught through the Passover; deliverance is taught through Israel being rescued from Egypt. Both Redemption and deliverance was accomplished through the shedding of blood and by the awesome power of God. As a whole, this book really instructs us that "obedience" to God is essential for a redeemed and set apart people.

At the outset of the book, we see the children of Israel crying intensely for relief, with God assuring their plea by developing Moses for this great purpose. Moses has a great encounter with God at the burning bush and he is told to go before Pharaoh as its leader.

Pharaoh demonstrates the severity of a callous heart's condition in his refusal to let God's people go in that he says, "Who is the Lord that I should obey His voice to let Israel go?" (Exodus 5:2).

Through a series of ten destructive plagues, God demonstrates His awesome power over Pharaoh and the gods of Egypt. Each plague increased in severity with the tenth plague bringing about death to the first born of every household in Egypt; but Israel is spared by means of the blood of the Passover lamb (Exodus 12:21-23). God further provides the basis for the Israelite's deliverance through the Red Sea after Pharaoh makes an attempt to pursue the frightened Israelites. Having crossed the Red Sea and being guided by God through a pillar of fire by night and a cloud by day, God continues to minister to His people by protecting and sustaining them in the wilderness. He feeds them manna in the morning and quail at suppertime.

In that hollering wilderness, God wants Israel to trust in Him each moment for their sustenance, as God wants us to do the same.

From chapters 1-18, you might say that the emphasis was upon "Israel's Rescue from Egypt." The latter half of the book (chapters 19-40), deals with "God's

Instructions for a Redeemed People." Having been delivered, protected, and sustained in the wilderness, God wants them to be set apart as a distinct nation. Moses is given the law on Mt. Sinai, with the law being the standard by which Israel was to distinguish herself from the world. Moses receives God's moral, civil and ceremonial laws, as well as instructions for the building of the tabernacle. The tabernacle was a building of elegance erected in the wilderness and portrayed much about the person of God and His way of redemption.

Leviticus

The author of Leviticus is Moses. He is the established leader that led the children of Israel from Egypt's bondage. Having been redeemed, the book of Leviticus instructs the newly redeemed priests on how to worship and serve God. This new group that departs from Egypt is now shown the manner by which they are to maintain a godly walk before God. There is an early principle set forth, "God saves us by faith through His Son's shed blood in order that we might walk worthy before Him."

As this book opens, we find the children of Israel in the wilderness for approximately one month at the base of Mount Sinai. In surveying the book, there is emphasis on the word "holy." In fact, Leviticus 11:45, says, "For I am the Lord who bringeth you out of the land of Egypt, to be your God; ye shall therefore be holy, for I am holy."

There is another verse that emphasizes holiness in Leviticus 19:2, which says, "Speak unto all the congregation of the children of Israel, and say unto them, ye shall be holy; for I the Lord your God am holy."

The apparent teaching of this book is how we should approach a holy God. Israel is instructed that approach unto a holy God is only through sacrifice by a priest, and that fellowship is maintained only through obedience evidenced by a pure walk. The person and work of Christ is taught in a dynamic way in this book. His person and work is seen through the five offerings: the burnt offering, meal offering, peace offering, sin offering and trespass offering. These offerings are symbolical of aspects of His sacrificial life that He offers as payment for our sin (Romans 3:24-25). We must remember that Christ paid the full payment for the ruin of sin.

Also, this book presents seven feasts that Israel is instructed to keep, and typifies some aspect of

Christ's redeeming work. The seven feasts are: Feast of Passover, Unleavened bread, First fruits, Pentecost, Trumpets, Day of Atonement and Tabernacles. In the book of Genesis, we see ruin through sin. In Exodus, we see redemption, but through Leviticus, we see worship.

Numbers

(Israel's Wilderness Experience)

As the book begins, it is a year since the children of Israel (God's people) left their slavery experience in Egypt. This book gets its name from the two numberings of God's children found in Numbers chapter 1 and chapter 26. The first is at Mt. Sinai and the next one is on the plains of Moab. It is a book which deals primarily with the wandering experience of Israel This wandering takes place because of their persistent murmurings, which evidence their lack of trust in God. Unbelief never promotes progress-it only hinders it!

God wants His people to walk by faith in route to the Promise Land and conquer it. The journey normally takes only eleven days. However, because of their failure to trust God, they wander aimlessly in the wilderness for forty painful years. There is a grave lesson for us in this book: "Unbelief forfeits Divine blessings."

Although they constantly murmur, God evidences His faithfulness to them, by leading them by the pillar of cloud and fire. He provides manna, water, and meat, and remains true to His covenant promise to them. He even furnishes them with a great leader in the person of Moses. God is indeed faithful to His people. However, He severely disciplines the old generation of Israelites that came out of Egypt (Numbers 14:29).

The sins of the people in this book are a vivid reminder to us that disobedience brings about swift discipline upon us when we persistently refuse to trust God. God certainly loves us but He will not tolerate our disobedient ways.

The tragic point of this book is that Moses and Aaron, great leaders of Israel, as well as the old generation which left Egypt, with the exception of Joshua and Caleb, never make it to the Promise Land (Numbers 14:22-23; 20:12). On a brighter note, this book offers several types of Christ. The bronze serpent in Numbers 21:4-9 pictures the Crucifixion of Christ. The reference to the "Rock" in Numbers 20:8,11 is a type of Christ's ability to satisfy our spiritual thirst.

The Manna in Numbers 11 is a type of Christ as the "Bread of Life" (St. John 6:35).

Overall, Israel does nothing but grumble along the way, yet God furnishes them with a sufficient diet in the wilderness. In closing, "We can only enter into God's rest as we trust in His superior way of guiding us."

Deuteronomy

Deuteronomy is a long discourse of Israel's leader, Moses, in which he gives messages to the new generation. Having survived the forty years in the wilderness, Israel is on the brink of occupying the Land of Promise, Canaan. Israel's long leader, Moses, is about one hundred and twenty years of age (Deut. 34:7). He leads Israel in an arid wilderness of forty years to the Plains of Moab. He forfeits the opportunity of leading them across the swelling Jordan because of his disobedience (see Numbers 20). God does allow Moses to view the Promise Land from the heights of Mt. Nebo, but he does not get the opportunity of taking the new generation across the Jordan (Deut. 34:1-5).

In our study of the book of Numbers, we glean a most vital principle: "Unbelief forfeits divine blessings!" Unbelief really prevents even Christians from receiving all that God has for us. This book, written by Moses, stresses the value of obeying God. Obedience is necessary if this new generation is to profit from the disobedience of their forefathers who left Egypt and died in the wilderness. In this book, Moses makes his last remarks by calling on this new generation to wholly trust God in order to receive His blessing. He exhorts them to learn from the "pitfalls of forgetting God" as they reach the Promise Land. Forgetting God leads to haughtiness and disobedience.

A verse that stresses the fact that Israel is not to forget God is found in Deut. 6:12, and it says: "Then beware lest thou forget the Lord, which brought thee forth out of the land of Egypt, from the house of bondage."

In the first half of the book (Deut. 1:1-4:43), Moses reminds the people that it was God who rescued them from Egypt's bondage, and sustained their forefathers in an arid desert. In the second half of the book (Deut.4:44-26:19), Moses calls the New Generation to covenant renewal. In essence, their existence as a nation depends on them obeying God's law. If they obey the law, then they will be blessed; however, if they disobey the law, they will be cursed (Deuteronomy 28). Finally, the last section of the book (Chapters 27-34), deals with Moses' final words to the nation. Moses is given a view of the Promise Land, but is not granted the opportunity of leading the new generation across the Jordan River.

The book ends on a sad note, for "The grand leader of Exodus does not become the leader of the Conquest." Although Moses is definitely saved, he does not fully receive all of God's blessings during his wilderness sojourn. What a tragedy!

Joshua

We come now to the first of the twelve historical books (Joshua-Esther), the book of Joshua, which serves as a transition from the leadership of Moses to that of Joshua. Joshua, an understudy of Moses, now assumes the leadership of guiding the people of Israel into Canaan. Moses, who dies at the age of 120 years (Deuteronomy 34:4-8) does not get the chance to lead the people across the Jordan River into the Promise Land because of his disobedience in wholly trusting in God before the people (Numbers 20:7-12).

If there is anyone who should lead the people across the Jordan into the Promise Land, it should be Moses! After all, Moses is the one who hears the people complain in singing the blues for forty years in an arid desert! The leader of the Exodus does not become the leader of the conquest.

In leading the people of Israel now, Joshua realizes that the success of his leadership is dependent on obedience to God. Great victories will be won through faith in God and obedience to His word, rather than through Joshua's military prowess or Israel's military supremacy! The theme of this book is Israel's occupation of the Promise Land.

The key verses of this book are found in Joshua 1:8 and Joshua 11:23, and they read – "This book of the law shall not depart out of thy mouth; but thou shalt mediate therein day and night, that thou mayest observe to do according to all that is written therein: for then thou shalt make thy way prosperous, and then thou shalt have good success." "So Joshua took the whole land, according to all that the Lord said unto Moses; and Joshua gave it for an inheritance unto Israel according to their divisions by their tribes. And the land rested from war."

The book of Joshua may be outlined as follows:

I. The Challenge in Conquering the Land of Canaan (Joshua 1:1-13:7)
II. The Division of the Land (Joshua 13:8-24:33)

Judges

In the book of Judges, we move from the period of "Conquest" to the period of the "Judges." Essentially, we move from the period of constant victory to one of continual defeat. In the book of Joshua, we see that as the people of God are obedient, they reap victory. However, in this book of Judges, we see that the people constantly disobey and they reap defeat. This book reveals how a nation departs from God's law and persists in doing their own will. Judges 21:25 says: "In those days there was no king in Israel: every man did that which was right in his own eyes."

By way of application, this verse informs us that whenever we depart from God's Word and set up our own standard for what is right, we go astray. Moreover, any nation that departs from God's Word, is doomed for failure and defeat. The spiritual temperature of the Nation of Israel is at an all-time low, as the people turn from the Word of God. God allows the enemies to oppress them. As the people cried out to God, God raises up a military leader (Judge) to throw off the oppression of the enemy.

The vicious cycle of departure, oppression and deliverance is constantly seen repeatedly in this book. When any people or nation abandon the Word of God, then that sin will leads to suffering. However, when a nation turns to God in repentance, God will hear and minister to that nation through His leaders. Sin in the heart of any nation must be dealt with by God, for Judges 2:20-21, says: "And the anger of the Lord was hot against Israel; and He said, Because that this people hath transgressed my covenant which I commanded their fathers, and have not hearkened unto my voice; I also will not henceforth drive out any from before them of the nations which Joshua left when he died."

As children of God during this dispensation of Grace, we must remember that when we sin, we must confess that sin and be restored unto God (I John 1:9). Remember, I John 1:9 is a verse for the Christian, not for the unsaved. The unsaved man must acknowledge Christ as his Savior (St. John 5:24, 3:36, Romans 10:8-9).

Ruth

The dark period of the Judges is marked by idolatry, immorality and unfaithfulness; whereas, the book of Ruth situated in the same period describes a Gentile woman's unusual faithfulness to Israel's God despite living in an unfaithful era.

The book of Ruth is an account of a Moabite woman, a Gentile, who abandons her pagan region (Moab) and embraces the God of Israel. Because of her unusual faithfulness, God blesses her by giving her a new husband (Boaz) and a son (Obed) and gives her the distinction of being in the lineage of David and Christ. Ruth marries Boaz and they become the great-grandparents of David.

The book opens with a famine in Bethlehem. Naomi's husband, Elimelech takes his family to Moab. There in Moab, he dies and his sons marry two Moabite women, Orpah and Ruth. The two sons eventually die, and Naomi is informed that the famine is over, and she decides to go home to Bethlehem. Naomi informs her daughters-in-law to remain in Moab and remarry. Orpah remains in the land, but Ruth decides to remain with her mother-in-law and embrace the God of Israel.

Her unusual demonstration of love and loyalty is seen in Ruth1:16, which reads: "And Ruth said, Intreat me not to leave thee, or to return from following after thee: for wither thou goest, I will go; and where thou lodgest, I will lodge: thy people shall be my people, and thy God my God."

Because of Ruth's steadfast loyalty to God, God providentially leads her to meet Boaz while gleaning in the field of Bethlehem. Ruth is greatly rewarded for her faith in God, for Boaz becomes her husband. One of the prominent principles of this book is that God will honor faith in Him. Another great principle in this book is that Gentiles are not outside the region of God's redemption. God will truly save those who place their trust in Him.

This book greatly teaches that one can live godly even in the midst of the prevalence of apostasy and immorality. Ruth's unfailing devotion to God is demonstrated during a time of great unrest and disturbance. Faith in Almighty God keeps us stable even in the midst of turbulent times. But, we must remain focused by looking to the object of faith – Jesus Christ (Hebrews 12:1-2).

Although Ruth lives during tough times, she remains loyal to her stance that she is going to follow her mother-in-law (Naomi) and embrace the people of Israel and their God. She forsakes her paganistic background, and embraces the true God – Jehovah. What great exhibition of faithfulness. She forsakes the world and follows the Lord. Is she rewarded? Yes, she is one of the few women (Tamar, Rahab, Ruth) who are included in Christ's lineage in Matthew, chapter 1.

I Samuel

The book of I Samuel tells about the change in leadership from the period of the Judges to the period of the Monarchy. The period of the Judges is marked as a time of no central government, and the people walked waywardly, for Judges 21:25, says: "In those days there was no king in Israel; every man did that which was right in his own eyes."

There are three outstanding persons in this grand book: Samuel, the last Judge and the first great prophet; Saul, Israel's first king; and David, the one anointed by Samuel to succeed Saul as Israel's second king. The author of this book of transition from the Judges to the Monarchy is said to be Samuel, although other scholars are in disagreement to the authorship of this book.

With Samuel being the key person in this period of transition, this book really describes the transition in leadership from a theocracy, where God is seen as the sole ruler, to a monarchy, where man is in rulership. Thus, we can see why the Nation of Israel is in a state of spiritual decline – they refused to follow God's rulership. A people or nation that persists to follow its own way, is subject to failure.

As Christians, we are better off as theocratic people, a people governed by the rulership of God. If we allow God to rule our hearts, we make better decisions when we are tempted in life. We can truly honor God and walk pleasing to Him if we only allow the Holy Spirit, who is within us, to have full control (Galatians 5:16). We need to follow God's rulership if we expect to receive His Divine approval!

As this book unfolds, God has a man who ministers during a turbulent time. Samuel's birth and call by God is described in Chapters 1-3. He readily responds to God's call during the period of corruption in the priesthood. Eli's infamous sons are guilty of corrupting the priesthood which leads to Israel's defeat in a battle with the Philistines (I Samuel 4:1-11). During this decisive battle, the Ark of God is taken. The Ark symbolizes God's presence among the people. God uses Samuel's prophetic mouth to bring revival, and the Ark is restored and the Philistines are defeated (Chapters 6,7).

However, after Samuel ages without having just sons to adequately lead Israel, the people clamor for a king like the other nations (I Samuel 8:5). Through God's permissive will, He allows the people to choose Saul as Israel's first king. Saul's reign begins well (Chapters 9-11), but ends in disaster, for he does three rather unwise things. In Chapter 13, he hastily acts in a priestly role that God did not sanction. In Chapter 14, he makes a foolish vow. Thirdly, in Chapter 15, he disobeys the Lord's complete command to utterly destroy the Amalekites. You might say, that three strikes and Saul was out!

From Chapters 16-31, even though Saul is still the king, David becomes Israel's new king. The rise of David's fame as a warrior in Israel causes Saul to be enraged with jealousy. Saul spends his time chasing David to kill him, instead of leading God's people as God directs him. He had the opportunity to lead God's people and did well at the beginning, but failed miserably at the end!

II Samuel

In I Samuel we see the rise and fall of Israel's first King, Saul. His failure came as a result of his inability to wholly trust God (I Samuel 13:13-15).

II Samuel details the reign of Israel's most illustrious leader, David. He reigns over Judah making Hebron his capital for about seven and a half years. Also, he reigns over all Israel, making Jerusalem his capital for thirty-three years. The date and setting of this book is sometime after the demise of Saul (931 B.C.) and before the decline of the Northern Kingdom to the Assryrian Empire in 722 B.C. or 721 B.C.

As Israel's great leader, David begins his career in 1011 B.C. and ends it in 971 B.C. Thus, David reigns as Israel's King for forty years. The book of II Samuel details the triumphs and troubles of Israel's leader, David. As with any great leader, there is always the danger of being tragically exposed by disobeying God.

After David's glorious triumphs recorded in chapters 1-10, we find him committing two gross sins: adultery and murder. From the point of committing adultery with Bathsheba in chapter 11, David reaps what he sows. He finds trouble permeating, not only in his home, but in the kingdom as well.

This book reminds us that "no one is exempted from the chastening hand of God" when one is wholly disobedient to God's will. God severely chastens even His most anointed leader. Great leaders can become victims of shame and disgrace if they are disobedient to God's will.

After David's great victories as Israel's valiant leader, the fame is soon displaced by his gross sin with Bathsheba. He never regains the glory and fame that he once possessed! However, he did acknowledge to God that he had sinned (Psalm 51), but he still has to "reap what he has sown" (Galatians 6:7). His most cherished son, Absalom, embarrasses David by wanting the kingship. The sword is still sharp in the home of David, for his son Amnon commits incest, and David's first child by Bathsheba eventually dies.

Nevertheless, David is described as "a man after God's own heart" because he has a faithful and repentant spirit (Acts 13:22). David did acknowledge and was very remorseful regarding his great sin with Bathsheba (Psalms 32, 51).

I Kings

From Devotion to God to Departure

Having viewed the reign of Saul (1051-1011 B.C.) and the illustrious reign of David (1011-971 B.C.), we come now to the glorious reign of the Nation's wisest and most celebrated king – Solomon (971-931 B.C.). The book of I Kings gives a striking account of the rise of Solomon, emphasizing his great accomplishments in leading the nation to the peak of its size and splendor. Solomon's greatest attainment was the building of the temple in Jerusalem. Although Solomon attained much wealth and amassed fame and glory as the nation's grand leader, his many foreign wives causes his heart to turn away from God.

Solomon begins his reign dedicated to wanting to lead God's people righteously. He even asks the Lord for wisdom in leading God's people. But his devotion to worshiping God is displaced when his many wives cause his heart to be turned away from God (I Kings 11:3-8). Solomon allows his wives to worship their own gods, which affects Solomon's total allegiance to God. It is ironic that the wisest man that God created acts so foolishly; and these foolish acts are committed during his latter days. There is a rather serious message that we can derive from Solomon's foolishness, and that is: "We need to order our steps according to God's word so as to prevent moral embarrassment."

In the first half of the book Chapters 1-11, we see the reign of Solomon to his tragic downfall. His marriages to foreign wives contaminate Solomon's worship of God thus, turning his heart from genuine worship of God. In the last half of the book Chapters 12-22, we see that after the demise and death of Solomon (931 B.C.), the United Kingdom is divided.

Rehoboam, the son of Solomon, does a foolish act of promising tough taxation upon the people. In revolt against this act, the majority of the people are led by Jeroboam, an official in Solomon's army. This revolt leads to the formation of ten tribes that follow Jeroboam, and the two remaining tribes (Judah and Benjamin) follow Rehoboam. After the division of the United Kingdom, there exists civil strife between the two Kingdoms, The Northern Kingdom and Southern Kingdom.

The most noteworthy kings of the Southern Kingdom in I Kings were Asa, Chapter 15 and Jehoshaphat, Chapter 22. All of the Northern kings in this book are wicked, especially Ahab. During Ahab's wicked reign in Israel, he introduces Baal worship. Jeroboam, the first king of Israel, is noted for introducing idolatry to Israel and making Samaria the capital for false worship. In conclusion, even during an age filled with demise and destruction, God often sends a ray of hope in the persons of Elijah and Micaiah. These prophets minister during this period admonishing the people to worship the true God.

II Kings

In I Kings, we see the sins which lead to the demise of both kingdoms, namely, immorality, idolatry and disunity. The nation of Israel, with its nineteen kings continues a course of disobedience, even in view of the persistent warnings of God's prophets. In 721 or 722 B.C., the Northern Kingdom falls to the Assyrians. The other Kingdom, Judah, lasts for over a century, yet she persists doing wrongly. Ultimately, Judah is taken in three deportations, 605 B.C., 598 B.C., 586 B.C. to Babylon. This results in Jerusalem being desolate and the temple is demolished.

The reason why Judah lasts longer is because Judah had some relatively good kings, in fact, there are eight of them. The most noted of the good kings is Asa, Hezekiah, and Josiah. Because of their godly influence, they are able to reform the vicious deeds brought about during the reign of a previous king. II Kings vividly details how disobedience and rebellion against God leads to the demise of both Kingdoms.

The prophets repeatedly warn the people and its rulers, but the rulers and the people do not heed the prophetic message of God. No nation can continue to spurn the message that God sends.

The Nation of Israel continues in the sins of its first king, Jeroboam, for II Kings 17:22-23 says: "For the children of Israel walked in all the sins of Jeroboam which he did; they did not depart from them, until the Lord removed Israel out of His sight, as He had said by all His servants the prophets. So Israel was carried away from their own land to Assyria, as it is to this day."

Judah did not reap a lesson from the tragic departure of Israel's going into captivity because II Kings 23:27 says: "And the Lord said, I will also remove Judah from my sight, as I have removed Israel, and will cast off this city Jerusalem which I have chosen, and the house of which I said, 'My name shall be there.'"

I Chronicles

A Sketch of David's Righteous Reign

Having gone through the political history of I Samuel to II Kings, First and Second Chronicles now gives a sketch of the religious life of David's dynasty of Judah. First Chronicles concerns itself with the kingly ruler of Judah's most illustrious king, King David, and shows the importance of his righteous reign.

As it relates to the author of First Chronicles, many scholars conclude that Ezra, the priest, is the writer; however, this cannot be proven with any degree of certainty. If Ezra is not the author, then many scholars conclude that a contemporary of Ezra wrote First Chronicles because of the book's priestly viewpoint. Mainly, the book's emphasis is on the temple and the priesthood during David's righteous reign in Judah.

This book covers many years of Israel's history from its inception to the conclusion of the Babylonian captivity. The message of this book reveals that God is indeed faithful to His people and that He has a purpose for them. This book teaches that although Israel goes into captivity and is disciplined, God is still among them. Although, there is no one sitting upon the throne of David, God is still actively among the people. Moreover, this book's message reveals that although the throne of David has vanished, the line of David will never vanish because the Messiah, Jesus Christ, will reign supreme in the future Millennium.

Important to this book is the Davidic Covenant of Second Samuel Chapter 7. This covenant is seen again in First Chronicles Chapter 17. It is true that Solomon fulfills part of this covenant, but its ultimate fulfillment is realized when Christ sits upon the earthly throne during the Millennium (Revelation 20).

As one glances at the events of Chapters 1-9, it is apparent that the author is giving a history of the Davidic dynasty (Southern Kingdom) with no concern for the Northern Kingdom (Israel). The genealogy shows that God is active in preserving a people for Himself from the beginning of humankind to the period after the Babylonian exile. The genealogical account in this section (Chapters 1-9) reveals that God is faithful in preserving His promises of keeping a Davidic line through many events of Israel's history. The last section of this book (Chapters 10-29) gives an account of David's illustrious reign as Judah's King.

Many of the events recorded in Second Samuel are not included in First Chronicles. First Chronicles omits many of the troubles that David encounters in his life. On the contrary, this book reveals the grace of God and His forgiveness that He offers despite the unfaithfulness of His people. The remnant coming home from the Babylonian Captivity needed to know that God in His grace can restore them.

The book closes with David making preparation for the building of the temple. Although, not granted the privilege of building it, he did have a desire to build it.

II Chronicles

The events of the book of Second Chronicles are somewhat similar to First and Second Kings, but with one exception. The Northern Kingdom (Israel) is ignored because of its false worship and its disdain for the temple in Jerusalem. Second Chronicles provides a vivid picture of the demise of the Southern Kingdom after the death of Israel's most famous and prosperous King, Solomon in 931 B.C. Furthermore, the content of Second Chronicles emphasizes the matter of constructing and dedicating the temple, for the temple was the center of worship. In the Old Testament, the temple symbolically stood for the presence of God among His people. This book provides great coverage to its construction and dedication, along with emphasizing also the priesthood.

One of the greater truths that this book teaches is that if God's people forsake Him, then He will withdraw His blessings, but not His presence. However, if God's people obey Him, then they will be victorious. As we explore the content of this book, one can easily see that it divides into two parts. In Chapters 1-9, the illustrious reign of Solomon is seen, and in Chapters 10-36, the reign of Judah's Kings are revealed. After Solomon's glorious reign, with the building of the temple and the expansion of Israel's borders, Solomon's glorious Kingdom begins to decline. The Kingdom splits after his death in 931 B.C. Second Chronicles gives a history of Judah's Kings, but great emphasis is placed on its eight good Kings: Asa, Jehoshaphat, Joash, Hezekiah, Josiah, Amaziah, Uzziah, and Jotham.

In Chapters 10-36, not only is the reign of Judah's Kings mentioned, but the book ends on a ray of hope.

In 538 B.C., Cyrus issues a decree which allows the Jews to return to Jerusalem to restore the temple. The temple's foundation is completed in 536 B.C., with the whole temple being completed in 516 B.C.

Ezra

With the opening of the book of Ezra, we are in the period of time around 538-458 B.C. in which a Jewish remnant makes their way back to Jerusalem after living in Babylon for seventy years. The book of Ezra gives an accounting of the remnant of people that return home to restore the temple. Under the spiritual leadership of Zerubbabel, the Jewish remnant returns home to rebuild the temple. The remnant makes their way home in 538 B.C. The remnant under Zerubbabel completes the foundation of the temple in 536 B.C., but because of opposition from the enemies of the land, the remainder of the temple is not completed until 516 B.C.

The book of Ezra gives a vivid account of how God fulfills His promise to restore the people to Jerusalem, for Jeremiah 29:14, says: "And I will be found of you, saith the Lord: and I will turn away your captivity, and I will gather you from all the nations, and from all the places whither I have driven you, saith the Lord; and I will bring you again into the place whence I caused you to be carried away captive."

This book shows that God indeed brings a remnant back to the land under the leadership and time of two great persons: Zerubbabel (538 B.C.); Ezra (458 B.C.). The book of Nehemiah gives an accounting of the last return from Babylon in 445 B.C. during which Nehemiah serves as the leader. The greatest teaching of this book is that after many years in Babylonian Captivity, God is indeed faithful to His word. This book gives every saint of God the courage to trust God in all circumstances in life, knowing "that all things work together for good to them that love God, to them who are the called according to His purpose." (Romans 8:28).

The book of Ezra stimulates us to trust God more knowing that His promises can never be frustrated by time.

Nehemiah

The background of the book Nehemiah takes place during the time of the Persian Empire period. The king reigning is Artaxerxes, the sixth monarch of the

Persian Empire. He begins his reign in 464 B.C. and Nehemiah, the chief character of this book, is serving as Artaxerxes' cup bearer (Nehemiah 2:1).

Nehemiah, the son Hachaliah (Nehemiah 1:1), is informed by his brother, Hanani, and other brethren from Judah that the walls of Jerusalem and the gates are in a state of ruin. Hearing of the condition in Jerusalem causes Nehemiah to become extremely sad, and in his state of distress, he prays to the God of Heaven (Nehemiah 1:4). The depressing news of hearing about the condition of Jerusalem leads Nehemiah to sincere prayer. This is a great principle that we can learn – mainly, that when we hear of depressing news about the situation of our day, we need to take it to the Lord.

Nehemiah responds to the gloomy news of the condition in Jerusalem by appearing before Artaxerxes requesting permission to go to Jerusalem in an effort to build the ravished walls (Nehemiah 2:1-5). Although Nehemiah feels extremely depressed about the situation in Jerusalem, he does not allow his sorrow to discourage him from positively doing something about the situation. He prays about the situation before he constructively acts to do something about it. Through prayer, careful planning and people working together, Nehemiah's project of building the ruined walls of Jerusalem is completed in fifty-two days (Nehemiah 6:15).

Esther

The portrait of Esther's life fits somewhere between the sixth and seventh chapter of Ezra, which occurs between the first return from Babylon led by Zerubbabel and the second return led by Ezra, around 536 B.C. and 458 B.C., respectively. This book of Esther provides the only biblical record of a vast segment of Jews who choose to remain in Persia, rather than return home to Palestine to rebuild the ravaged city of Jerusalem after the exile. Although the name of God does not appear in the book, His providential concern and protection is apparent throughout the book. Although God's name is not mentioned, He is working behind the scene achieving His intended results through ordinary people, who being used by Him accomplish great things to God's glory.

The book opens with a feast given by King Ahasuerus (Xerxes) during his third year as King of Persia in 483 B.C. History reveals that the purpose of the banquet is to plan for his military campaign against Greece. Having been defeated by the Greeks in 479 B.C.,

Herodotus, the historian, discloses that Xerxes seeks comfort in his harem.

At his winter palace in Susa, Ahasuerus uses this occasion to showcase the beauty of Vashti, then Queen of Persia. When she refuses to appear, and because of her impudent behavior, Vashti is deposed as Queen, with the highly favored one, Esther, replacing her. Rising to a position of prominence, Esther is counseled by her Uncle Mordecai not to reveal that she is a Jew.

In the first half of the book (Chapters 1-4), we see how God providentially works the events of this book to bring Esther to the position as Queen. One of the apparent truths of this book is that God has a plan for everyone's existence.

Although Esther is in a position of prominence as queen of Persia, she remains in contact with her Uncle Mordecai, and through her help she reveals to King Ahasuerus of a plot against the King's life. In the meantime, Haman instigates a plot to exterminate all Jews because of Mordecai's refusal to bow to him.

In fact, through this plot, he convinces the King to issue an edict to have all the Jews in the province slain. In an effort to spare the Jews' lives, Mordecai reveals to Esther that God placed in a privileged position for a purpose. The memorable verse that details God's purpose in raising her to a position of power is found in Esther 4:14, which says, "For if thou altogether holdest thy peace at this time, then shall there enlargement and deliverance arise to the Jews from another place; but thou and thy father's house shall be destroyed: and who knoweth whether thou art come to the kingdom for such a time as this?"

In the second half of this book (chapters 5-10), we see that God intervenes to deliver His people. Instead of Haman having the Jews slain, Haman is hanged on the gallows prepared for Mordecai (Esther 5:14, 7:10). Thus, with this deliverance, Mordecai rises to a position second only to the king.

The feast of Purim is instituted which serves as an annual reminder of God's steadfast faithfulness on behalf of His people. In the book of Esther, we have discovered that God used ordinary people to accomplish an extraordinary feat; and that God certainly has a plan for our lives.

Job

The author of the book of Job is unknown. This dramatic account of the trials of Job is unusual in its depth. The setting probably takes place during the patriarchal times of Abraham, Isaac, or Jacob. If so, the book of Job is one of the oldest books in the bible. Scholars suggest that Moses is the author or even Job himself. The fact that Job is a real historical figure is confirmed by both Ezekiel and James (ref. Ezekiel 14:14, 20; James 5:11). The book of Job unveils the disaster of a blameless saint (Job 1:1) who loses everything including his wealth, family, health and his societal respectability.

Job is in an awful dilemma. Suddenly, He goes from fortune to misfortune. The natural question surfaces – "Why does the Lord allow disaster to strike the life of an innocent man?" Although Job suffers severely in this book, God does not tell Job the "why" of his disaster. After the trying experience of suffering, Job's theology concerning God changes dramatically. God is not obligated to answer the "why" in any situation in life. It is apparent that the debate in heaven (Chapters 1-2) between God and Satan culminates in Job's plight. Moreover, Job's plight prompts his friends to present lengthy arguments regarding his dilemma (Chapters 3-37). In their discussion with Job, Job magnifies his self-righteousness in defense of himself. In reality, these friends do not help Job, their dialogue brings out more of Job's self-righteousness. Job's friends insist that Job is guilty of some sin due to the fact that he is suffering. Job feels that these friends are judging him and dismisses them all as unworthy comforters as stated in Job 16:2 – "I have heard many such things; miserable comforters are ye all."

After Job's discussion with his friends and Elihu's dialogue, God Himself silences the debate by speaking from the whirlwind. God interrogates Job by asking him a series of potent questions about nature. Job is reduced and he repents. The book closes with Job praying for his friends and being restored. God doubles his wealth and gives him the same number of children. Job realizes through God's questioning of him in Chapters 38-42 that God is sovereign and He is in complete control over everything. If suffering is permitted in life, it is for the saint's own good and for God's glory.

Psalms

One of the most instructive sections of the Bible is the book of Psalms. The contributing authors to Psalms are David, who many scholars believe penned at least seventy-three Psalms; Solomon, who wrote two; Asaph, a Levite director of David's choir, who wrote twelve; Korah family of singers, who wrote twelve; and others.

Their time of authorship spans from about 1410B.C. to 430 B.C. The word psalm, many scholars believe, means a composition to music. Thus, the Psalms were set to the accompaniment of stringed instruments and were used in the temple as the saints worship God. They were also used as a hymnbook for the people of God, the Jews.

As one reads the various Psalms, one will gather that the writer is reflecting some circumstance in which he is undergoing or the Jewish people. Most of the Psalms are expressing the fact that God is worthy of worship because of "Who He is." They stress that God is to be extolled because of "What He has done." In fact, no other Old Testament book instructs as much about God.

In the various Psalms, the great attributes of God are enumerated, such as His omnipotence, omniscience, omnipresence, eternity and His immutability. Psalm 8 brings out the fact that God's name is to be exclaimed and praised; the psalmist is even overwhelmed as he views God's creation and ponders why man is being considered by Him.

Man, the capstone of God's creation, certainly has worth and is endowed with dignity. Every man has value because he is the object of God's unconditional love and concern. The Son of Man, Jesus Christ, came down from heaven on a missionary trip to save man who had fallen in the Garden of Eden through Adam and Eve, when they partook of the forbidden fruit, thus causing all men to be born unsaved. Jesus Christ made that missionary Journey from heaven and inhabited a body like man, yet without sin, and died on a rugged cross and was buried but rose triumphantly from the grave for sinful mankind.

The book of Psalms is divided into various divisions, with each division corresponding to the Pentateuch section of the bible with Psalms 1-41 corresponding to the book of Genesis; Psalms 42-72, Exodus; Psalms 73-89, Leviticus; Psalms 90-106, Numbers; Psalms 107-150, Deuteronomy. Thus the individual Psalms are not referred to as chapters.

Finally, many scholars have classified the various Psalms into six categories. Penitential Psalms ask for God's forgiveness (Psalms 32, 38, 51). Acrostic Psalms have verses or sections beginning with succeeding Hebrew alphabetic letters (Psalms 25, 119, 145). Hallelujah Psalms praise Jehovah or contain the word "Hallelujah", which means praise the Lord (Psalms 146-150). Imprecatory Psalms reveal the vindictive attitude of the psalmist toward his enemies and call down a curse (Psalms 35, 69, 109). Historical Psalms present important historical events in poetic form (Psalms 78, 105, 114). Prophetical Psalms tell of coming events including the coming and eventual reign of Christ (Psalms 22, 69, 110).

If you need to know how to walk worthy for Him, read Psalm 1. If you need to be encouraged as you experience hardships, read Psalm 3. If you need proper guidance from the best counselor the world has ever known, read Psalms 23. If you need the Lord to illuminate your path as you face the evil encounters of life, read Psalm 27. And if you need an answer as you face the various problems of this life, read Psalm 73. Finally, if you want to know the Psalmist extreme value of God's word, read Psalm 119.

The psalmist had a high regard for God's word, for in Psalm 119:11, 97 says: "Thy word have I hid in mine heart, that I might not sin against thee . . . O, how I love thy law! It is my meditation all the day."

Proverbs

Solomon, the son of the illustrious David, is the principal author of Proverbs. The key word of Proverbs is wisdom, the ability to live life skillfully. Proverbs is a book that instructs believers how to live successfully in an ungodly world; thus Proverbs is God's manual for His people in living a godly life as they confront the various issues of everyday life.

Solomon is regarded as the wisest man to ever live. At the outset of his glorious reign as King of Israel (971-931 B.C.), he asked the Lord for wisdom so that he could lead the nation and to adequately judge between right and wrong (I Kings 3:6-12). God grants his request, giving him a wise and discerning heart with more wisdom than anyone before him and anyone who is born after him. The famed Queen of Sheba makes known that Solomon is indeed endowed with wisdom (I Kings 10:1-8).

According to I Kings 4:32, Solomon spoke three thousand proverbs and one thousand and five songs. From Solomon's many proverbs, only about eight hundred or more are included in the book of Proverbs. The book of Proverbs can be viewed as a collection of maxims that deal with the practical affairs of everyday life.

Solomon and the other authors are covering from the book of Proverbs a number of subject matters that include: wisdom, folly, pride, humility, love, hate, laziness, wealth, poverty, justice and vengeance. Reading the various Proverbs may take a couple of minutes; but to apply these precepts, one needs the Holy Spirit's guidance! The theme of Proverbs is found in Proverbs 1:7, which says: "The fear of the Lord is the beginning of knowledge: but fools despise wisdom and instruction."

To fear God means to reverence Him; thus such a reverence should lead one to trust Him by humbly depending upon Him. A person is truly wise when he honors God through his daily walk. The precepts presented in this book, if practiced, will give every believer the skills necessary to maintain a righteous walk before God. If these sage precepts are practiced, it will help the believer evade the pitfalls of moral embarrassment or shame. If advice is needed on the right company to keep, read Proverbs 1:15-16 "My son, walk not thou in the way with them; refrain thy foot from their path: For their feet run to evil, and make haste to shed blood."

If one is searching for wisdom (skill for living), Proverbs 2:6 says - "For the Lord giveth wisdom: out of His mouth cometh knowledge and understanding."

This book even reveals the path to a healthy spiritual life, Proverbs 3:5-6 says – "Trust in the Lord with all thine heart; and lean not unto thine own understanding. In all thy ways acknowledge Him, and He shall direct thy paths."

The book of Proverbs provides the instruction to guard against the adulteress (Proverbs 5:1-6); and how to avoid laziness (Proverbs 6:6-11). Instruction is even given in disciplining children, Proverbs 13:24, says: "He that spareth his rod hateth his son: but he that loveth him chasteneth him betimes."

In connection with that verse on disciplining children, Proverbs 23:13-14, says – "With hold not correction from the child: for if thou beatest him with the rod, he shall not die. Thou shalt beat him with the rod, and shalt deliver his soul from hell."

There are more verses in this book that are instructive to parents in rearing their children found in Proverbs 29:15, 17 – "The rod and reproof give wisdom: but a child left to himself bringeth his mother to shame. Correct thy son, and he shall give thee rest; yea, he shall give delight unto thy soul."

Proverbs concludes with a portrait of a godly woman, in Proverbs 31:10-31. Of particular note is verse 30 –

"Favor is deceitful, and beauty is vain; but a woman that feareth the Lord, she shall be praised."

Ecclesiastes

The author of the book of Ecclesiastes is Solomon, the wisest, richest and most influential king of Israel. It is commonly agreed by biblical scholars that Solomon wrote this book during the latter part of his existence, probably around 935 B.C. Solomon died in 931 B.C. Right after his death, United Israel split, with two tribes going to the South; thus, we call those tribes Judah; and ten tribes going to the North, of which we call those tribes Israel. Solomon penned this book during a time when his glorious reign was disappearing, when his glory was fading.

The preacher, Solomon, is glancing at "life under the sun" and concludes from a human perspective that life is empty and futile. In his quest "under the sun", he sought power, wealth, pleasure and prestige as a means of happiness and satisfaction, only to experience a total void and empty and frustrating end. This book's ultimate teaching is that man will never find real meaning and satisfaction apart from his creator – God.

Man, the capstone of God's creation, is so constituted by God and will never be ultimately satisfied until he finds his satisfaction in God. Man must take full advantage of his opportunity in life to get related by faith to the only source of true contentment and joy – Jesus Christ. True meaning and purpose in life is not found in pleasure, wealth or fame but is found in the only person who can give eternal life, as Jesus Christ states in St. John 10:28 – "And I give unto them eternal life; and they shall never perish, neither shall any man pluck them out of my hand."

Solomon's frustration is caused by him trying to understand life "under the sun" and not from God's perspective. Whenever we try to view life "under the sun", with life's many inequities, uncertainties and injustices, it only leads to utter emptiness and despair. But, wisdom comes when we start glancing from a Divine perspective and begin to wholly trust in God in the face of the many absurdities, difficulties and perplexing issues of life. There are many issues of life that we are not able to comprehend, but as we look beyond the now, and by faith, trust that the Sovereign Creator is working everything for our good, for Romans 8:28 says "And we know that all things work together for good to them that love God, to them who are the called according to His purpose."

In conclusion, after Solomon's quest to find happiness and satisfaction through pleasure, wealth, prestige, and power, he comes to a settled resolve that the whole duty of man is to "fear God, and keep His commandments: for this is the whole duty of man. For God shall bring every work into judgment, with every secret thing, whether it be good, or whether it be evil" (Ecclesiastes 12:13-14).

The Song of Solomon

The Song of Solomon is a courtship of love and eventual marriage of King Solomon to a beautiful woman of no means, the Shulamite. Many commentators view this story as the greatest of Solomon's songs (1:1), for the bible says that Solomon wrote 1,005 songs (I Kings 4:32). The book, Song of Solomon, was probably written by Solomon about 965 B.C.

From a historical point of view, this book depicts God's great love for Israel as His espoused bride (Hosea 2:19-20) and the church as the bride of Christ. This book describes the wooing of love between a Shulamite peasant woman and King Solomon, with a chorus (daughters of Jerusalem) in the background. Similarly, God's great expression of love for sinful mankind is clearly in the sending of His Son, Jesus Christ; and it is climatically demonstrated on a rugged hill called Calvary, where Christ suffers on a cross of shame for six hours. What a genuine description of man's extreme hatred for God; but what a mighty depiction of God's absolute love for man.

The book of the Song of Solomon is a poetic expression of Solomon's genuine love for a Shulamite woman. The key verses of this book are found in Chapter 7:10 and 8:7, - they read "I am my beloved's, and his desire is toward me." "Many waters cannot quench love, neither can the floods drown it: if a man would give all the substance of his house for love, it would utterly be contemned." Verse 7 is very instructive, for it says that genuine love cannot be stopped or put out, nor can it be purchased; but it can be expressed.

God's inexplicable love (agape love) is shown in Christ making a missionary trip from heaven to die for sins of human kind. His great love was exhibited not to a deserving humanity, but an undeserving one, for Romans 5:8 says, "But God commendeth His love toward us, in that, while we were yet sinners, Christ died for us."

Truly, the dramatic love story of the Song of Solomon is a picture of God's undying love for His covenant people, Israel and His anticipated union between Christ and His Church. After Solomon wins the affection of this Shulamite woman of beauty (1:1-5:1) and marries her, he takes her to his palace in Jerusalem. She is disturbed by a dream of Solomon knocking at her door, but she answers too late; thus Solomon has departed (5:2-8:14). In his return, he tells her of his love and extols her beauty (6:4-7:10).

This great love story concludes with the bride making her journey back to her homeland, but the couples' love for each other is not diminished, for chapter 8:14, says –"Make haste, my beloved, and be thou like a roe or to a young hart upon the mountains of spices."

As believers in this church age, and depicted as the bride, we have been separated from the bridegroom for over 2,000 years, but one day we will be forever united with Him (Revelation 22:20).

Isaiah

Isaiah is commonly called the "evangelical prophet" because of his explicit and thorough messianic prophecies. He ministered from 740 B.C. to 680 B.C., during the reign of four kings of Judah – Uzziah, Jotham, Ahaz and Hezekiah (Isaiah 1:1). This great prophet of God is from a noted Jewish family, educated, having a wife and children. Yet, he is dedicated to the task of proclaiming God's message with a stern conviction, and displays a sincere and compassionate heart for the people. The book of Isaiah is really a miniature bible within itself. The first thirty-nine chapters are similar in tone to the theme of the thirty-nine books of the Old Testament, stressing the righteousness, holiness and justice of God.

The second half of this book, chapters 40-66, is similar in tone to the grand theme of the twenty-seven books of the New Testament, stressing the glory, compassion and grace of God. Isaiah's name means "Yahweh is salvation." The word "salvation" is often used in this book, and this book is the most quoted book in the New Testament.

Some key verses of the book of Isaiah are found in Isaiah 9 and Isaiah 53 – "For unto us a child is born, unto us a Son is given; and the government shall be upon His shoulder; and His name shall be called Wonderful, Counsellor, The Mighty God, The Everlasting Father, The Prince of Peace. Of the increase of His government and peace there shall be no end, upon the throne of God, and upon His Kingdom, to order it, and to establish it with judgment and with justice from henceforth even for ever. The zeal of the Lord of hosts will perform this" (9:6-7). "All we like sheep have gone astray; we have turned everyone to this own way; and the Lord hath laid on Him the iniquity of us all" (53:6).

In the first half of the book (Chapters 1-39), Isaiah is proclaiming that God will indeed judge Judah, the surrounding neighbors of Judah, and the world for its iniquity because of God's righteous character of holiness.

During the ministry of Isaiah, the dominant power of that day was Assryia, which increased in power under Tiglath-pileser (745-727 B.C.). As Assryia conquers the small nations around the Mediterranean coast, even threatening Judah, Isaiah vehemently exhorts Judah's kings not to form an alliance with foreign countries to thwart Assryian invasion, but to trust wholly in God's power. In 701 B.C., Judah is miraculously delivered from Assyrian invasion by Sennacherib.

In the second half of the book, the theme changes from condemnation (chapters 1-39) to consolation (chapters 40-66). This section portrays a suffering Savior who atones for the sins of the people (Isaiah 53). This rejected Savior suffers but is exalted. At His first coming, He came to suffer, but at His Second Coming, He is coming back as the Sovereign King and will usher in a kingdom of peace and righteousness throughout the earth.

Jeremiah

The prophet Jeremiah is divinely directed by God to proclaim an unwelcomed message of judgment to the nation of Judah (the Southern Kingdom). It is a stern message of judgment that God placed upon Jeremiah, because the people are engaged in such intensive sins as apostasy, idolatry, and distorted worship. Because of these sins, the nation is declining spiritually. In view of such moral depravity, God calls upon Jeremiah to inform the people to repent because immediate judgment lies ahead. Because of Jeremiah's faithfulness in proclaiming God's message, he is subjected to being persecuted and rejected by the enemies of the message, as well as, his own familiars.

Although Jeremiah is opposed, beaten, hated, persecuted and even imprisoned, he nevertheless, remains faithful to God. He is unpopular and the object of maltreatment. But, he in love for God's people, continues to proclaim God's message in spite of the adverse conditions of his time. He is not afraid to speak out for God about the prevailing moral ills of Judah.

Jeremiah, a tender man, yet also a man of sternness, is noted as the weeping prophet. He proclaims the messages that God gives him in love for over forty years (627 B.C. – 580 B.C.). No doubt, Jeremiah knew to expect opposition from the priests and prophets of Jerusalem, but not from his own hometown people.

This book teaches ministers that when you proclaim the message of God with the intensity of a Jeremiah, you will experience rejection. Jesus Christ, a greater than Jeremiah, also is severely rejected by His own hometown people (John 1:11). Although Jeremiah preaches a message of doom, he also preaches a message of hope.

Lamentations

Lamentations is a portrait of the devastating results of what sin caused. Sin does bear fruit; and this book depicts its fruitfulness in the thorough destruction of the once proud city, Jerusalem. This book was no doubt composed by Jeremiah. The time of the writing of this grand funeral dirge is perhaps 586 B.C. This book is perhaps the most mournful books of the bible – wherein Jeremiah is expressing his compassion and tender grief over the destruction and desolate condition of Jerusalem. The once proud city of Jerusalem – the temple, palace and walls – were now reduced to ruin.

The ministry of Jeremiah, a contemporary of Zephaniah, Habakkuk, Daniel, and Ezekiel extended to Judah from 627 to about 580 B.C. He faithfully exhorts the erring nation that their only recourse is to submit to God's instrument of correction – the Babylonians – because judgment is soon to occur. Because of Jeremiah's unwelcome messages, he is often mistreated by his countrymen by being rejected, despised, beaten and even imprisoned. Yet, he remains faithful to the task to which God gave him. He is fearless in his pursuit to proclaim what "thus saith the Lord." Now, Jeremiah must witness to Jerusalem's holocaust; now his heart-stirring messages are breaking his tender heart, because he is witnessing to the very devastation that he prophesied would happen!

In five funeral dirges, Jeremiah is giving to us a graphic portrayal of the complete ruination of the once beautiful city of Jerusalem. As an instrument of God's corrective rod, Babylon laid siege of Jerusalem from 588 B.C. to 586 B.C., finally conquering this once elegant city in 586 B.C. In five funeral dirges, Jeremiah is expressing his untold sympathy for the desolation of the city and for the captives deported to distant Babylon. Now, Jerusalem lies in rubble, with no prophets, priests or kings; no temple, palace or people.

In spite of the bleak period of misery, Jeremiah is about to rise to a summit of hope. How is he about to rise from utter helplessness and hopelessness to one of majestic hope? In the midst of the prophet being heartbroken, Jeremiah expresses his deep seated faith in the goodness and mercy of God, for Lamentations 3:22-23 says – "It is of the Lord's mercies that we are not consumed, because His compassions fail not. They are new every morning: great is thy faithfulness."

As believers we go through some valleys of dark hardships but through it all, our future looks radiant and full of hope. It is never as bad as it seems. Jeremiah is able to transform a tragic situation to a summit of faith by trusting God, One who has been faithful in the past, faithful now, and will be faithful in the future. Although the nation has to go to distant Babylon for seventy years, on a brighter side, God did promise that the nation would be restored. In times of difficulties, this book teaches that God is faithful, for He always works in harmony with His consistent character.

Ezekiel

Ezekiel, who ministered during the dark and decadent days of Judah, was a contemporary of both Jeremiah and Daniel. He was of priestly descent (Ezekiel 1:3) and his name means "God strengthens." A resident of Jerusalem, he is later deported to Babylon in 597 or 598 B.C. during the second deportation of Judah to Babylon. There were three deportations of Judah to distant Babylon, namely, 605 B.C., 598 B.C. and 586 B.C.

As a prophet of the Lord, Ezekiel's task is to instruct Judah before her exile that her sins precipitated God's judgment on them. However, Ezekiel also brings a message of consolation that God's future blessing with regard to His covenant will be fulfilled. Thus, the theme of this book is similar to the other prophets. In the first half of the book, we see the "condemnation" section (Chapters 1-32), with the second half, we see the "consolation" section. In the first section, Ezekiel outlines the sins that initiated God's judgment upon the people and to reveal the folly of Judah embracing any hope of returning home before the seventy years of captivity. In other words, God's judgment on Judah is surely to happen and her captivity will not be brief; she will spend seventy years in Babylon (Jeremiah 25:11-12). Not only is Judah indicted and will soon be punished (Chapters 1-14), but Judah's surrounding nations (the Gentiles) will be severely judged also.

In this book, Ezekiel's exhortation to the people of Judah came in the form of signs, messages, visions and parables. Having gone to Babylon during the second deportation (598 B.C.), Ezekiel ministers to the captives by the river Chebar, assuring them that although Jerusalem has fallen, God will not terminate His covenant promise of future blessing and complete restoration. God's people will be restored to the land of Jerusalem. What a comforting thought.

This book teaches us that God must judge sin, but He makes provision for His people to return to Him.

One of the most interesting Chapters of Ezekiel is found in Chapter 37 – "the Valley of the Dry Bones." In this vision, the nation is described as lifeless, dry bones. Although lifeless, God reassembles them and breathes life into those bones! Just as He is able to bring life to the dead nation of Israel, He can save any unsaved man who is "dead in trespasses and sins" (Ephesians 2:1).

Daniel

The Apocalypse of the Old Testament

This book provides a noble approach to prophetic history. The book of Daniel portrays four successive Gentile world powers (Babylon, Media-Persia, Greece and Rome), and will demonstrate their rise and declension, paving the way for the coming of our great King – Jesus Christ.

The writer of this book is Daniel, whose name means "God is my Judge." Many biblical scholars are in agreement that he was deported to Babylon, maybe around the age of sixteen, and that his deportation was around 605 B.C., along with his three Hebrew companions (Daniel 1:6-7). Scholars also agree that Daniel is one of the few spotless characters found in the bible – with the other ones being Joseph and Samuel. Daniel and his three companions are men of unusual faith, for their faith in God is certainly put to the test; and in each trial in which their faith is tested, they emerge as victorious.

This book demonstrates that God does not abandon His people and that faith in Him is rewarded. These men are not in Jerusalem; however, they remain loyal to the God of heaven in a godless culture.

As stated this book provides a panoramic view of four Gentile world powers, and it also provides us with the fact that our God is reigning in the affairs of men, and He exalts and deposes kingdoms as He wills. No doubt, this book was written to exhort the exiled Jews by unfolding to them God's sovereign program for Israel during and after the "times of the Gentiles" domination.

The times of the Gentiles begin with Babylon, a time in which Israel is without a king (Luke 21:24). During this period, Israel suffers under these world powers, but God does not abandon Israel. The theme of this book is encouraging because it discloses that

God is sovereign and will triumph over human powers. God, the great presider of human history, has not deviated from His intended program. Many great powers have come and gone, but our God is in sovereign control in human affairs.

The outline of the book of Daniel is as follows: The life of Daniel described (Chapter 1); God's Prophetic Program for the Gentiles (Chapters 2-7); God's Prophetic Program for Israel (Chapters 8-12). In chapter 1, after Daniel's remarkable demonstration of faith is tested and it triumphs, Daniel is unusually used by God to interpret dreams in which God's prophetic program for the Gentiles is outlined. Through Daniel's interpretive ability, God reveals the way in which He will raise and depose of four world powers. God allows the powers to operate for only a short while, but in the end, He is acknowledged as the "Supreme One".

The prophetic history for the Nation of Israel is outlined in chapters 8-12, with the encouraging words that: "the saints of the Most High shall take the kingdom, and possess the kingdom for ever, even for ever and ever" (Daniel 7:18).

Hosea

Hosea, a contemporary of Amos in the Northern Kingdom, and Isaiah and Micah of the Southern Kingdom, began his illustrious career during the reign of Jereboam II. Hosea, whose name means "salvation," ministered primarily to the Northern Kingdom during a time when she delighted in political and economic prosperity. However, on a spiritual level, the Northern Kingdom was declining, guilty of committing such sins as lying, murder, insincerity, ingratitude, idolatry and covetousness. Hosea was the husband of Gomer and the father of three children with prophetic names: Jezreel (God Scatters); Lo-Ruhamah (Not Pitied); Lo-Ammi (Not My People).

Hosea is given an unusual command by God to marry Gomer, a woman who is obviously unstained before the marriage, but becomes guilty of committing adultery during the marriage. Thus Hosea's personal marital issue becomes an accurate depiction of Israel's unfaithfulness to God, for like Gomer, Israel too becomes unfaithful to God, despite the Lord's faithfulness to her. In other words, just like Gomer was unfaithful to Hosea, Israel was unfaithful to God.

Meanwhile, Hosea demonstrates his love and compassion for Gomer by redeeming her from the slave market (Chapter 3). Likewise, the Lord demonstrates His unconditional love for Israel in His plea to her to turn back to Him, for Hosea 14:1 says – "O Israel, return unto the Lord thy God; for thou has fallen by thine iniquity."

Hosea had the arduous task of presenting a passionate message of judgment to the erring nation; however, he tempered his message with concern and compassion for his people. This book can be outlined as follows:

I. An Adulterous Wife – Chapters 1-3;

II. An Adulterous Nation Judged And Later Restored – Chapters 4-14.

In Chapters 1-3, the tragic marriage of Hosea is illustrated with Hosea redeeming his adulterous wife from the slave market. This act demonstrates Hosea's love for Gomer, and richly illustrates the Lord's unconditional love for Israel, despite Israel's pursuit of other lovers.

In the last half of the book, Chapters 4-14, Hosea's intense pain in his marital situation provides him with much understanding of the pain and grief God experiences over the sins of His people. Because of the nation's refusal to heed God's gracious appeals to repent, the nation must undergo massive corrective discipline in the form of judgment. Because of the Lord's hesed (loyal) love, the nation will be restored. The Lord must punish sin, but because of His ceaseless love, He will greatly save His people and restore His erring people.

Some verses that are power-packed which demonstrate the Lord's unusual hesed (loyal) love and concern for His wayward people are found in Hosea 11:8 and Hosea 14:4, which read: "How shall I give thee up Ephraim? How shall I deliver thee, Israel? How shall I make thee as Admah? How shall I set thee as Zeboim? Mine heart is turned within me, my repentings are kindled together." "I will heal their backsliding, I will love them freely: for mine anger is turned away from him."

Joel

Joel, a prophet during the reign of Joash (Jehoash) (835-796 B.C.) describes a severe locust invasion in Judah, and he uses this traumatic event as an illustration of the coming Day of the Lord which will bring judgment to those who do not trust in the Lord. Although the locust invasion is a devastating event, it will pale in comparison to God's coming judgment upon Judah because of Judah's sins.

The Day of the Lord is depicted in scripture as a time beginning with the tribulation period, and it extends through the Millennium (thousand year reign of Christ). Thus, it is an extended period of both cursings and blessings; cursing upon those who spurn God's offer of salvation through Jesus Christ; and blessings upon those who trust the Messiah – Jesus Christ. This book conveys the thought that the only "hope" for Judah is sincere repentance before this awful event (Day of the Lord) occurs. In that day, God will certainly bring judgment upon His enemies, but blessings upon those who trust in Him.

The theme of this book stresses the sovereignty of God in human history, for its theme is in keeping with the name of Joel, which means "Yahweh is God." It is comforting to know that the courses of nature and nations are under God's control. God is directing the affairs of this life, not man!

Christ came down from the heights of heaven to dwell among men through the incarnation process. He came the first time to emancipate man from the ills of sin, for man was in dire need of a Savior. Christ, the God-man, became man's substitute – dying upon an old rugged cross for all mankind. As mankind's only hope for entrance into heaven, Jesus died as man's expiatory sacrifice for sin; a death that fully satisfied the justice of Almighty God.

The book of Joel can be outlined as follows:

> I. The Awful Day of the Lord Illustrated (Chapters 1:1-20);
> II. The Day of the Lord in the Future (Chapters 2-3).

God will certainly vindicate His righteousness in the future Day of the Lord when He judges mankind for his rejection of His offer of salvation. Our Saviour came as the matchless Lamb of God during His first advent; but during His second advent, He is coming to judge mankind. Mankind can accept Him as the Lamb of God now, or refuse to accept Him and face Him as judge. As mankind's only hope, He will preside at all of the future judgments, for St. John 5:26-27 says – "For as the Father hath life in Himself; so hath He given to the Son to have life in Himself; And hath given Him authority to execute judgment also, because He is the Son of man."

The list of all judgments that our Savior will preside over, along with the scriptural references is as follows: The Judgment of the Believer's Works (Church) (I Corinthians 3:11-15; II Corinthians 5:10); The Judgment of the Gentiles (Nations) (Matthew 25:31-46; Joel 3:2); The Judgment of Israel (Ezekiel 20:37-38); The Judgment of Fallen Angels (Jude 6, I Corinthians 6:3); The Judgment of the Unsaved Dead (Revelation 20:11-18). Accept Christ now as your sufficient Savior, or meet Him as the awful Judge. He has a right to judge; because as Son of Man, He died for mankind.

Amos

The book of Amos is among the Minor Prophets in the Old Testament. Amos prophesied during a period of extreme bounty in Israel. Business was abounding and Israel's boundaries were extending and were flourishing. Yet, beneath a period of remarkable growth, the nation was guilty of such sins as – empty ritualism, greed, materialism, oppression of the poor, injustice and arrogance. In the midst of Israel's external growth, the nation's internal growth was waning, for Israel was guilty of insincerity in her worship of God and developed an attitude of feeling secure, thus becoming more and more indifferent to God's hand of correction.

Against this background of national opulence and stark indifference to the chastening hand of God, stood this rustic prophet/preacher of Tekoa. With a style of being stern and having a resolute desire to fulfill his divine commission to proclaim, Amos rebukes the social sins of the nation, warning them that God's judgment is imminent; thus, the Nation needs to repent of its social ills to avert God's judgment. Amos, a resident of the south-Tekoa (Tekoa was in Judah – twelve miles south of Jerusalem), yet he preaches to the Northern Kingdom (Israel).

Amos' message of judgment seems ridiculous, largely because the nation is experiencing prosperity which produces a false sense of security and an optimistic outlook. Amos, whose name means "burden" or "burden bearer," lives out the true meaning of his name by bearing under the great load of declaring to a callous nation that "God's judgment is pending."

This verse, "prepare to meet thy God" (Amos 4:12), is speaking about Israel's need to prepare to meet God in judgment because they refuse to repent. Amos preaches a stern message of judgment, announcing the coming doom of Israel, resulting in the captivity of Israel to the Assryians in 722 B.C., the prophet also proclaims a message of hope, with the blessings of David's line being reinstated and the promise of the people being restored to their land (Amos 9:11-15).

Although the great majority of the book's message centers around "judgment" (Amos 1:1-9:10); there are several verses that depict hope (Amos 9:11-15). In the midst of immorality, false religious ritualism, injustice and material prosperity that breed a false sense of security, there is a ray of hope that is found only in the most central figure of history – Jesus Christ.

Obadiah

The Destruction of Edom

Obadiah is a book in the Minor Prophet section. The Minor Prophets wrote in brevity; whereas, the Major Prophets wrote more at length; yet, the Minor Prophets are no less inspired by God than the Major Prophets. This book is about an event concerning twin brothers, Esau and Jacob, whose family feud, really a struggle that began in the womb, culminates in a national hatred that exists among their respective descendants (Genesis 25:21-33).

The struggle within the womb of Rebekah (Isaac's wife) anticipated the struggle between two nations (the Edomites and the Israelites). The younger brother (Jacob) would occupy the premier position over the older brother (Esau).

In Genesis chapter 25:31-32, Esau sold his birthright to satisfy his physical hunger; thus, this act alone displays Esau's regard for spiritual things. He forfeited his spiritual blessings for temporary pleasure. In Genesis chapter 27, Esau was deceived in a scheme concocted by his mother, Rebekah, and implemented by his brother, Jacob, in securing the family blessing. Thus Esau had forfeited his birthright and was deceived of the family blessing.

With this background in mind, a national struggle between two nations, the Edomites and Israelites is conceived. The descendants of Esau are the Edomites; the descendants of Jacob are the Israelites. That enmity is further seen in the Edomites' callous indifference and hatred in rendering aid to Israel during the time of her wilderness sojourn (Numbers 20:14-21). The Edomites refused vehemently in allowing Israel passage through their land enroute to Kadesh.

And that enmity heightens in this book with Obadiah (whose name means "worshiper of Yahweh") condemning the Edomites for treating Judah so cruelly in a time of her greatest need when the Babylonians were invading Jerusalem in 586 B.C. The Edomites displayed their fierce enmity against Judah by joining the enemy in the destruction of Jerusalem. The Edomites even rejoiced and participated in the looting of Jerusalem by the Babylonians.

In the first half of this book (v.1-18), Obadiah enunciates the certainty of Edom's judgment, a judgment so certain because of Edom's pride (v. 3). The Edomites felt a sense of security because they lived in the mountainous region of Mount Seir. But Obadiah prophesies their total overthrow by God for the Edomites maltreatment of her brother (Judah) (v.10-14).

In the second half of the book, Obadiah announces the restoration of Israel (v. 19-21). God will judge the Edomites in the day of the Lord (v. 18) and Israel will possess her own land, as well as the land of Edom and

Philistia. There are four vital principles that we should learn from this book:

(1) Be aware of pride. Pride is the leading cause of having a false sense of security. The book of Proverbs tells us about pride, for Proverbs 16:18 says – "Pride goeth before destruction, and an haughty spirit before a fall."

(2) Be cautious of how you treat your brother. Hatred is the leading cause of family feuds. We need to love people unconditional as God does, for St. John 3:16, says – "For God so loved the world, that He gave His only begotten Son, that whosoever believeth in Him should not perish, but have everlasting life."

(3) God will certainly judge mankind. He judged Edom for her maltreatment of Judah (v.15). He also will judge mankind for refusal to accept the only hope for mankind, Jesus Christ. "He that believeth on Him (Jesus) is not condemned: but he that believeth not is condemned already, because he hath not believed in the name of the only begotten Son of God" (John 3:18).

(4) Be aware of the many false means of security. There is only one true means of security

today – Jesus Christ. Only those who are secure in Jesus Christ are really secure.

Jonah

"A Prophet Who Didn't Like His Assignment"

Jonah, the only prophet commissioned to preach directly to the Gentiles, was from a place called Gath hepher, which was three miles north of Nazareth in lower Galilee; thus, Jonah was a renown prophet of the Northern Kingdom. His name means "dove".

According to II Kings 14:25, Jonah was a prophet during the reign of Jereboam II, king of Israel. During his reign, Israel experienced prosperity and national pride prevailed. But during Israel's national fervor, the formidable power of the Assryian Empire was gradually growing. The Assryians were notoriously cruel in their barbaric treatment of their captives, often flaying their victims to demonstrate their prowess in overcoming and defeating their enemies.

With this background in mind, Jonah refuses to obey God's missionary command to preach repentance to the cruel Assryians! Jonah allows his nationalistic fervor of his nation to blind him from having compassion for the cruel Assryians. But also, Jonah knows that God is a God of mercy and that if Nineveh responds aright to God's message of repentance, that God will spare the Ninevites.

As the book unfolds, Jonah is called to preach repentance to the wicked Ninevites. The Lord has instructed him to go the Ninevites (northeast); yet, Jonah went west to Tarshish (Spain). Jonah knows that God is a God of mercy and that if Nineveh responds in obedience, then God will extend His mercy and spare the Ninevites from judgment. Thus, Jonah does not want to be viewed as a traitor to his nation. Having received the commission from God to be a foreign missionary to the cruel and barbaric Assryians (Jonah 1:1-2), Jonah disobeys and goes to Tarshish. Jonah goes west, but God instructs him to go northeast.

As a result of his disobedience, Jonah is judged by God on the sea and he is eventually engulfed in a fish. It is ironic that the things of nature obey God, but God's foreign missionary doesn't. Certainly, disobedience leads to judgment and Jonah's disobedience causes havoc for others associated with him on the sea.

Having disobeyed God (Jonah 1:3), Jonah now becomes devotional (Chapter 2). In the depths of that great fish, Jonah pours his heart out to God in thanksgiving, for he was delivered from being drowned (Jonah 2:9). When God orders the fish to vomit Jonah on dry soil (Jonah 2:10), Jonah no doubt reflects on his experience of being incarcerated as he begins to make his five hundred mile journey northeast to Nineveh. God is sovereign and He controls the events of life. His plans cannot be opposed by mere mankind,

God provides Jonah another opportunity - "God gives us second chances." In Chapter 3, we find Jonah in God's will, doing exactly what God him to do in the first place (Jonah 3:3). So, Jonah is no longer a disobedient (Jonah 1:3) prophet, but now he is declaring prophet (3:4). He preaches a one-sentence message and his message achieves unbelievable results. Jonah's one-sentence sermon brings about a great revival in Nineveh, for the king of Nineveh proclaims a fast and the city repents. Thus, God spares the city.

In Chapter 4, instead of being elated with the success of his preaching, the prophet becomes highly displeased and even wishes to die (4:8). But God is tender with this despondent missionary. Jonah is thankful that his life is spared but highly despondent that God spared the hated and despicable people of Nineveh.

In the last part of this book, Jonah falls in love with a castor-oil plant (gourd) which the worm devours the next morning (4:7). Jonah has more love for the plant than for people. God has a grave message to be observed, "people are God's greatest concern." God's supreme passion is that men be saved, for II Peter 3:9, says – "The Lord is not slack concerning His promise; but is longsuffering to us-ward, not willing that any should perish, but that all should come to repentance."

Micah

Micah, a pre-exilic prophet, was a country preacher who was called from the town of Moresheth Gath (Micah 1:14), located about twenty-five miles Southwest of Jerusalem. He was a contemporary of Hosea in the Northern Kingdom and of Isaiah in the Southern Kingdom. According to Micah Chapter 1:1, he prophesied during the reign of three kings of Judah; Jotham (739-731 B.C.), Ahaz (731-715 B.C.), and Hezekiah (715-686 B.C.).

This rustic preacher had an intense concern for the social welfare of the people. The poor people of Judah were suffering immensely from the well-established and influential populous of Judean society. The infiltration of evil had permeated every level of social society and Micah voiced his concern regarding it.

During Micah's prophetic ministry, the priests were ministering for avarice (greed) and not for Almighty God. The princes committed and dominated its populace with cruelty, violence and extreme corruption. The landlords were cheating under privileged and evicting the widows; the businessmen were using crooked weights and scales, thus, exploiting the poor. The prophets were preaching for wealth, not for the spiritual development of the people.

Against this dismal background of fraud and corruption, stood this fearless denunciator of evil – Micah. In this brief, but yet important Minor prophet book, Micah details the sins of the nation, sins that will plummet the nation to destruction and captivity. But in the midst of the bleak period of social injustice, there is a ray of hope.

The only hope for the prevailing condition of inequity is the climactic appearance of the Divine deliverer – Jesus Christ. His reign alone will put an end to social evil, for He will reign in righteousness and true equity. This is also the only hope to the prevailing sin condition of depraved mankind. Any man who is outside the ark of Christ needs a spiritual remedy. Jesus Christ is the only hope for the sinful condition of depraved man.

The book of Micah can be outlined as follows:

> (1) Micah's denunciation of the sins of the nation (Chapter 1:1-3:12)

> (2) Micah's declaration of the Restoration of the Nation (Chapter 4:1-5:15); God's appeal to repent (Chapter 6:1-7:20).

In the first section of this book (Micah 1:1-3:12), Micah is denouncing the sins of both Israel (Samaria) and Judah (Jerusalem). Both kingdoms will be captured and go into captivity because of their rampant evil. Judgment is imminent and the nation must be punished.

In the second section of the book (4:1-5:15), Micah's prophetic message shifts from judgment to restoration. There is hope for the nation, for the coming redeemer will appear in the person of Jesus Christ. A remnant of God will be preserved and the kingdom will be instituted. In the last section of the book (Chapters 6:1-7:20), we are introduced to a court scene, wherein God is calling on the hills and mountains to be jury witnesses as He pleads His case against the nation. God's case against the people is obvious, for the people were guilty of substituting genuine worship with baseless ritual, and really thinking that such hypocritical actions were pleasing to God.

Micah declares what God demands in Micah 6:8, for it says – "He hath shewed thee O man, what is good; and what doth the Lord require of thee, but to do justly, and to love mercy, and to walk humbly with thy God?"

Nahum

The book of Nahum presents a startling message of judgment issued by God's prophet, Nahum. Nahum, whose name means "comfort" or "consolation", is a prophet called upon to issue a stern message of judgment to Assyria for her habitual sins of violence, idolatry and pride. Assyria really thought that her walled city made her impregnable and invincible, but it was no defense against the impending judgment of Almighty God. God's patience with this once proud city had been exhausted; there was nothing but judgment to be decreed upon Assyria; it was inescapable.

Therefore, Nahum's message is laced with judgment upon the immoral and cruel Assyrians. They were spared a century ago (760 B.C.) through the preaching of Jonah when they repented, thus Assyria experienced a citywide revival. Now, a century later (660 B.C.), Assyria had reverted to its old sinful habits, and God's patience had been exhausted. There was nothing but judgment to be issued upon a privileged nation. Now, Assyria stood ripe for judgment because she had forgotten her revival and had degenerated to her former sinful habits of immorality and utter cruelty. Assyria will be overthrown by the Babylonians in 612 B.C.

A thought from this minor prophet book is "Consistency with God's Justice and Holy Character requires that He must judge sin. He loves the sinner, but sin is repulsive to God's character."

Nahum's message of judgment on Assyria, served as a message of comfort to Judah. Assyria would be destroyed for its violence against the nations and its arrogance against God. At the outset, we see that Assyria had the privilege of experiencing a revival in response to the preaching of Jonah, only to discover that it was short lived. Now having been so privileged (St. Luke 12:48), Assyria had succumbed to her immoral ways of idolatry and cruelty. What is God left to do? Judgment is imminent.

Habakkuk

Very little is known about this minor prophet, Habakkuk, whose name means "embrace" or "clings". Habakkuk ministered during the declining time of Judah, just before Judah was deported to Babylon in 605 B.C. His prophetic ministry probably was during the reign of a godless king of Judah by the name of Jehoiakim (609-597 B.C.). Thus, Habakkuk began his prophetic ministry about 607 B.C.

During the time of his ministry the stubborn and callous-hearted people of Judah were guilty of violating God's law, which was manifested with the escalation of violence and injustice prevailing. Viewing the mounting evils of his day caused Habakkuk to raise some grave questions to God –

questions that revealed that Habakkuk was struggling in his faith.

There are times when all of us have doubts in the way things are being dealt with in society today – especially when conditions around us seem to be getting worse, not better. Habakkuk struggled with the issue of injustice prevailing and seemingly nothing was really being done about it. Because of the prevalence of violence and injustice in Judah, Habakkuk directs three piercing questions to God:

(1) Why are the wicked advancing and flourishing among God's people?

(2) Why are the righteous being trampled upon?

(3) And why is God seemingly unresponsive to the prevailing evil in the land?

To these perplexing questions, God answers by announcing to Habakkuk that He is doing something, for He will send the mighty Babylonian army to punish lawless Judah (1:5-11). God's first answer (1:5-11) to Habakkuk's first severe question (1:1-4), will cause this perplexed prophet to raise an even more serious question – "How can God who is supremely holy and pure allow someone as Babylon who is more wicked that Judah to chastise God's people?" (1:12-2:1).

As you see, Habakkuk is dealing with a very tense issue, an issue that promoted him to doubt the way in which God was operating the affairs of life! From a watchtower, God answers this bewildered prophet (2:2-20) by informing him that "the just shall live by faith" (2:4). This expression, "the just shall live by faith" is repeated three times in the New Testament (Romans 1:17; Galatians 3:11; Hebrews 10:38), for its truth is in agreement with the doctrine of justification by faith.

When conditions around us are so overwhelming to the extent that inequities are prevailing, we need to rely on our faith, knowing that God is on the throne, ruling in the affairs of men. Genuine faith in God will safeguard us from crumbling in the sea of despair –coasting with confidence in God even during the adverse conditions of our day.

So, what do we need to keep us stable, even during a turbulent period of uncertainty? We need to know that God is working out the fine details of life, working according to His perfect plan (Romans 8:28). This book began with Habakkuk being perplexed by the existence of violence and injustice parading in Judah and God was seemingly indifferent regarding it. But the book will close by Habakkuk praising God, rather than posing questions to Him.

So in the first half of the book, we observed a troubled prophet (1:1-2:20). However, in the latter half of the book (3:1-19), we will observe a triumphant prophet. This same prophet who was perplexed, is now praising God, for Habakkuk 3:19, says: "Yet, I will rejoice in the Lord, I will joy in the God of my salvation."

Habakkuk discovered that you can always trust in God, even during the difficult moments of life. In the end, Habakkuk began to affirm that God can be trusted because of His goodness, wisdom and power. This book is a theodicy, which is a firm defense of God's goodness, wisdom and power even in the midst of evil. The more that you "trust the planner, the less you will doubt His plan."

Zephaniah

The book of Zephaniah should capture our attention, for it was written during the splendid reign of King Josiah around 625 B.C. During the illustrious reign of Josiah, Zephaniah brought about a revival. However, that revival only engendered an outward change for the most part in the conduct of Judah, but did not permanently remove the inward perversion of the hearts of Judah. With unrelenting fervor,

Zephaniah will forcefully exclaim that the Day of the Lord is imminent when the Lord will judge Judah and the devastation of sin will be severely wiped out. God's wrath will come and no one can suppress His judgment against sin.

Sin is like a malignant cancer that must be dealt with and only God can cure mankind of the deadly effects of sin. Sin is the cause of the turbulence and restlessness we are experiencing in the world today and only God can cure America and other countries from the devastating effects of sin. God has a remedy for such mounting problems as war, racial discord, or even the social diseases in our land.

One portion of scripture that offers the cure is found in II Chronicles 7:14, which says – "If my people, which are called by my name, shall humble themselves, and pray, and seek my face, and turn from their wicked ways; then will I hear from heaven, and will forgive their sin, and will heal their land."

God has the cure but mankind must receive the medicine to be cured that God's word offers. The root of man's problem stems from the fact that man inherited a malignant problem called sin. Because of our forefather's initial sin in the Garden of Eden (Genesis 3:6), mankind has been affected by the devastating perils of sin. Sin is the cause of all the evil that pervades our society. But there is a cure for the sin-sickness of our land. Mankind must turn to the Lord in repentance and receive God's only cure for the sin-sickness of man in Jesus Christ, for St. John 14:6 says – "I am the way, the truth, and the life: no man cometh unto the Father, but by me."

There are many preachers/pastors who are pouring out God's word in this age, exclaiming that Judgment Day is coming, get prepared to meet God! Zephaniah was doing the same in his age. On the whole, this book is a grim reminder that God's judgment is imminent; however, at the close of this book, Zephaniah reveals that there is a ray of hope for Judah and the nations in that God promises restoration (3:14-20).

This book can be outlined as follows:

I. God's Wrath Revealed in the Day of the Lord (1:1-3:8)
II. God's Wonderful Salvation Included in the Day of the Lord (3:9-20).

What is the most crucial message that we can derive from the book of Zephaniah? Mankind needs to repent earnestly before God to avert God's judgment, for every man will appear in court before God – whether he or she is covered in God's righteousness through faith in Jesus Christ or uncovered because of stubborn refusal to accept God's only substitute for sin – Jesus Christ.

Haggai

At this juncture of the Old Testament, we are in the post-exilic period (the period after the exile of the Jews from Babylon), wherein the Jews have made their trek back to their homeland (Jerusalem) in an effort to rebuild the desolate temple. The Jews were granted permission by the Persians to go home to rebuild the temple in 538 B.C. The Jews began the project of rebuilding the temple but they were met with opposition from the enemies within.

With sixteen years having elapsed since they started the project, the Jews began to build their own ceilinged homes and virtually neglected the completion of God's business of finishing the temple. They were guilty of having misplaced priority – putting their own affairs before God's business. Against this background of spiritual neglect, came the fiery ministry of Haggai urging the people to finish the work of rebuilding the temple. As a contemporary of Zechariah the prophet, Haggai begins his ministry about 520 B.C. with the primary task of stirring the people to finish building the temple. Haggai's name probably means "festival" or "festive" and he probably came from the remnant of Jews that came from Babylon.

Cyrus, king of Persia, issued the decree in 538 B.C., ordering the Jews to go back to their homeland with Zerubbabel, the governor, leading the group. The work of rebuilding the temple started, but it was not completed. Having read about the awesome task Haggai faced with urging the people to complete the job started, and the blessings they forfeited as a result of their own spiritual lethargy, one arresting thought can be seen – "God's people must complete God's business, or face the result of missing God's blessings in their lives."

The key verses of this book are found in Haggai 1:7-8, and Haggai 2:7-9, and these verses read – "Thus says the Lord of hosts; Consider your ways. Go up to the mountain, and bring wood, and build the house; and I will take pleasure in it, and I will be glorified, saith the Lord" (1:7-8). "And I will shake all the nations, and the desire of all nations shall come: and I will fill this house with glory, saith the Lord of hosts" (2:7-9).

Through the fiery ministry of Haggai, the people resumed the work and the temple was completed about 516 B.C. (Ezra 6:14-15). As God's servant for the hour, Haggai had to encourage the Jews to resume the work they had started and he stressed in this book that God requires holiness and obedience of life from His people, for sin in the life of His people will hinder God's blessings.

This book begins with Haggai urging the people to finish the construction project of rebuilding the temple, but it ends on a much higher note. Haggai exclaims complete confidence in the future with the coming of the Messiah to rule the nations of the world, for Haggai 2:20-23 says – "And again the word of the Lord came unto Haggai in the four and twentieth day of the month, saying speak to Zerubbabel, governor of Judah, saying, I will shake the heavens and the earth; And I will overthrow the throne of kingdoms, and I will destroy the strength of the kingdoms of the heathen; and I will overthrow the chariots, and those that ride in them; and the horses and their riders shall come down, every one by the sword of his brother. In that day, saith the Lord of hosts, will I take thee, O Zerubbabel, my servant, the son of Shealtiel, saith the Lord, and will make thee as a signet: for I have chose thee, saith the Lord of hosts."

Zechariah

Zechariah, a contemporary of Haggai, and a post-exilic prophet, was commissioned by God to encourage the Jews to rebuild the temple. The work of rebuilding the temple had started in 536 B.C., but because of opposition from the enemies within, that work had ceased. Through the encouraging ministry of Zechariah and the urgent proclaiming of Haggai, the temple was rebuilt finally in 516 B.C. (Ezra 6:14-15).

Instead of using powerful words of rebuke, Zechariah stimulated the action of the people by reminding them of the future importance of the temple – namely, the Messiah's glory will be present in it. In every age, God has effective leaders as Zechariah, one who gets the job done by not forcing his will upon the people, but by showing the people the importance for the work that is being done.

Zechariah's name means "God remembers". He was probably born in Babylon and came to Palestine when a number of Jewish exiles came from Babylon in 538 B.C. under the leadership of Zerubbabel. The book of Zechariah has been called "the major minor prophet" because it has the longest section of the minor prophets. Moreover, in this book, there are many Messianic passages, but two familiar ones are found in Zechariah 8:3 and Zechariah 9:9, and they read as follows: "Thus says the Lord: I will return to Zion, and dwell in the midst of Jerusalem. Jerusalem shall be called the city of truth, the Mountain of the Lord of hosts, the Holy Mountain" (Zechariah 8:3). "Rejoice greatly, O daughter of Zion! Shout, O daughter of Jerusalem! Behold, your King is coming to you; He is just and having salvation, lowly and riding on a donkey, a colt, the foal of a donkey" (Zechariah 9:9).

This book can be outlined as follows:

I. Encouragement While Rebuilding the Temple (Chapters 1-8).
II. Instructions in View of Anticipating the Arrival of the Messiah (Chapters 9-14)

The book of Zechariah discloses God's future plans for His covenant people (Israel), and it progresses to a major climax with the coming of the Messiah in splendor and glory as the great conqueror over the nations as He delivers His people, Israel. The Messiah in His second advent will reign in Jerusalem over the entire world (Chapter 14).

Malachi

Malachi's historical setting was during a time of the Persian domination of Judah, a period between 539 B.C. and 333 B.C. Malachi's name means "My Messenger." Although little is known about this prophet of God, many scholars believe and advance that he actually proclaimed the message of this book during the period between 432 B.C. and 425 B.C. The book was primarily addressed to Judah, denouncing some flagrant sins such as covetousness, idolatry, mixed marriages with foreign people, and mistreating the poor. These are some of the same sins that Judah was guilty of which brought about her captivity to Babylon.

With a degree of stern denunciation, Malachi pronounces God's judgment against Judah during a time of extreme corruption among the priests and the unduly and wicked practices of the people. Because of Judah's incessant rebellion, evident in her callous heart, Malachi proclaims God's curse upon those who engage in the wicked practices of the nation. The people of Malachi's time were living so wickedly until they became insensitive to sin. Their prevailing attitude was that serving God was useless, for their way of thinking was evident in their wicked practices. The people wanted to receive God's blessings;

however, Malachi will reveal that God's blessings will be realized only when the people wholeheartedly repent.

In every dispensation, repentance has always been the foundation for receiving God's blessings. There are several key verses in this book which will aid one in grasping an understanding of the book of Malachi, and they are: Malachi 2:17, 3:1, and 4:5-6. In definite order these verse read – "you (ye) have wearied the Lord with your words, yet ye say, Wherein have we wearied Him? When ye say, Every one that doeth evil is good in the sight of the Lord, and He delighteth in them; or Where is the God of Judgement?" (Malachi 2:17). "Behold, I will send my messenger, and he shall prepare the way before me: and the Lord, whom ye seek , shall suddenly come to His temple, even the messenger of the covenant, whom ye delight in: behold he shall come, saith the Lord of host" (Malachi 3:1). "Behold I will send you Elijah the prophet before the coming of the great and dreadful day of the Lord: And he shall turn the heart of the fathers to the children, and the heart of the children to their father, lest I come and smite the earth with a curse." (Malachi 4:5-6).

Malachi predicts that Elijah will appear before the day of the Lord, with that prediction being partially fulfilled in the coming of John the Baptist, a forerunner of Jesus Christ. With the closing of the book of Malachi, there is a period of four hundred years of silence in which there is no word from heaven. Many scholars refer to this period of four hundred years of silence as the "Intertestamental Period." This silence is broken with the arrival of John the Baptist, the forerunner of Christ, with these arresting words – "Behold the Lamb of God, which taketh away the sin of the world." (St. John 1:29).

Whereas, the book of the Genesis begins with creation, the book of Malachi will conclude with a curse. The book can be outlined this way:

I. The Special Advantage of the Nation (Malachi 1:1-5)
II. The Wicked Practices of the Nation (Malachi 1:6-3:15)
III. The Coming of the Lord Predicted (Malachi 3:16-4:6)

As stated before, this book closes with a curse because of the persistence of sin on the part of the people, which is made evident for the arrival of the Messiah.

The New Testament

A Brief Outline of the Life of Christ

I. His Birth Through Age 30
    A. Bethlehem (birthplace) Luke 2:4-7
    B. Jerusalem (around two years old) Matthew 2:1-12
    C. Jerusalem (age 12) Luke 2:42-52
    18 years of silence perhaps working as a carpenter.
    D. Baptism (start earthly ministry, age 30) Luke 3:21-22

II. His Ministry Age 30 through 33
    A. Selection of Disciples, later called Apostles Luke 6:12-16
    B. Three-fold Ministry (Teaching, Preaching, and Healing) Matthew 4:23

III. His Passion
    A. Upper Room Discourse (Discourse before His demise) John 13-17
    B. Apprehension – Garden of Gethsemane Luke 22:40-46; Matthew 26:36-45; Mark 14:32-42
    C. His Trials – Six Kangaroo Courts
        1. Three Jewish
            a. Annas John 18:12-14

        b.   Caiaphas   Matthew 26:57-68

        c. Sanhedrin Matthew 27:1-2

    2. Three Roman

        a. Pilate John 18:28-38

        b. Herod Luke 23:6-12

        c. Pilate John 18:39-19:6

D. Severe Suffering Experience

    1. Crucifixion Mark 15:25; John 19:17-37

    2. Burial Mark 15:42-47; John 19:38-42

IV. His Resurrections & Post-Resurrection Ministry

    A. His Resurrection Mark 16:1-8; Luke 24:1-12; St. John 20:1-9

    B. His Resurrection – Many Infallible Proofs Acts 1:1-3

    C. His Ascension Acts 1:11

A Brief Study of the Holy Spirit

Part I

One of the more neglected subjects of the bible is the subject regarding the Holy Spirit. Not only has the subject been neglected, but there is much confusion with regards to the Holy Spirit's person and work. In this study, you will view a brief question and answer study regarding the Holy Spirit. Listed below are some of the questions and answers with reference to the third person of the Eternal Godhead.

I. In the scriptures, what is the Holy Spirit declared to be?

The Holy Spirit is declared to be a Person, rather than an influence. He is revealed as being equal in deity and attributes with the Persons of the Godhead. He is the third Person of the Godhead. (Genesis 41:38; Exodus 31:3, 35:31; Numbers 27:18; Job 33:4; Psalm 139:7).

II. Was the Holy Spirit active in the Old Testament?

Yes, His activity in the Old Testament was that of coming upon different people in the Old Testament to accomplish different objectives, and then leaves them when the work is completed. (Judges 3:10; I Samuel 16:13).

III. When did the Holy Spirit come into the world in an abiding sense?

On the day of Pentecost, the Holy Spirit abode in every believer.
(Acts 2)

IV. Does the Holy Spirit indwell every believer? What scriptures support your answer?

Yes, the moment an unsaved person believes the gospel, he or she is indwelled by the Holy Spirit. (John 7:37-39; Acts 11:15-17; Romans 5:5; Romans 8:9-11; I Corinthians 6:19-20).

V. Does the Holy Spirit withdraw His presence from a child of God when he has sinned?

No, the Holy Spirit never leaves the child of God. On the other hand, the child of God should confess all known sins so that the Holy Spirit can work in an effective way in his life. The Holy Spirit abides in the heart of a believer forever. (John 14:16).

VI. Can a believer quench the Holy Spirit?

Yes, the Holy Spirit is quenched by not yielding to the revealed will of God. (I Thessalonians 5:19).

VII. Does the Holy Spirit glorify Himself or whom?

No, the Holy Spirit glorifies the Son, Jesus Christ. (John 16:14).

Part II

Continuing from Part I of this study we will now look at the Seven Main Ministries of the Holy Spirit.

The seven main ministries of the Holy Spirit are:

I. The Ministry of Restraining. II Thessalonians 2:6-8. The Holy Spirit is presently holding back the forces of evil. There is a restraining power in the world and it is evidently one of the present ministries of the Holy Spirit.

II. The Ministry of Reproving the World of Sin, Righteousness and Judgment (John 16:7-11).

A. The unbeliever is made to understand that the sin of unbelief in Jesus as his personal Savior is the one sin that stands between him and salvation.

B. The Holy Spirit informs the unsaved that Christ is the perfect illustration of the righteousness of God. This includes the fact that God is a righteous God who demands much more than human accomplishments as basis for salvation but faith in Christ is the only basis for salvation. More important, the Spirit of God reveals that there is a righteousness available by faith in Christ and that when one believes in Jesus Christ he can be declared righteous, justified by faith, and accepted by his faith in Christ, who is righteous both in person and in His work on the cross (Romans 1:16-17; Romans 3:22, 4:5).

C. The Holy Spirit also illuminates the unsaved that the work on the cross is finished, that judgment has taken place, that Satan has been defeated, and that salvation is available to those who put their trust in Christ.

III. The Ministry of the Holy Spirit in Regenerating. When one places their trust in Christ, he is said to be regenerated by the Holy Spirit (John 3:6) and has become a legitimate child of God. He has partaken of the divine nature and Christ is begotten in him "the hope of Glory."

IV. The Ministry of the Holy Spirit as Indwelling. The Holy Spirit indwells every true believer the moment he places trust in Christ (I Corinthians 6:19-20; Romans 8:9-11; I Corinthians 2:12; Romans 5:5, I John 3:23).

V. The Ministry of the Holy Spirit in Baptizing. The Baptizing of the Holy Spirit is the organic placing of the believer into the body of Christ, it is that operation of God which establishes every position and standing of the Christian (I Corinthians 12:13).

VI. The Ministry of the Holy Spirit in Sealing. The ministry of the Holy Spirit in sealing evidently represents the God-ward aspect of the relationship – authority, responsibility and final transaction. The Holy Spirit is the seal and all who have the Spirit are sealed. The sealing is the divine mark that secures the believer until the day of redemption (Ephesians 4:30; II Corinthians 1:22; Ephesians 1:13). The sealing of the believer is actually God's ownership of the believer.

VII. The Ministry of the Holy Spirit in Filling. To be filled by the Holy Spirit is to be controlled by the Holy Spirit (Ephesians 5:18).

The Biblical Resurrections

St. John 5:28-29; I Corinthians 15:20-23

As we approach this lofty study on the resurrection, it is a fundamental fact that all men (from Adam to the last man who dies) will eventually be raised from the dead, although they will not be raised at the same time. The statement just uttered has scriptural validation, for St. John 5:28-29 says, "Marvel not at this: for the hour is coming, in the which all that are in the graves shall hear His (Christ's) voice, And shall come forth; they that have done good, unto the resurrection of life; and they that have done evil, unto the resurrection of damnation."

Clearly, from these verses, we can establish that there are two groups: (a) the righteous of all ages who will experience being raised to the resurrection of life, though at different times; (b) the unrighteous ones, the wicked of all ages, will be raised to a resurrection of damnation; in fact, all of the wicked dead will be raised at the same time after the millennium (Revelation 20:5) to stand before Jesus Christ, the One they rejected, at the Great White Throne (St. John 5:27; Revelation 20:11-15).

Our blessed Lord will preside at all future judgments, for St. John 5:27, states, "And hath given Him (Christ) authority to execute judgment also, because He is the Son of man."

The resurrections as taught in the Bible should be studied in relation to the future judgments, because all men are raised to be judged; our Lord was judged and then raised. So, why should any man experience the agony of going to hell when Christ has sufficiently paid the price of God's wrath against sin, when He offered Himself on Calvary's cross for my sins and yours?

Mankind can be rescued from the plight of spending an eternity in the lake of fire by believing in the gospel (the death, burial and resurrection of Jesus Christ – I Corinthians 15:3-4). Because of our Lord's triumphant victory over the grave, every believer of all ages who dies is assured that he or she will be raised, though not at the same time. There are definite orders to the biblical resurrections, for I Corinthians 15:23, says: "But every man in his own order: Christ the first fruits; afterward they (the righteous of all ages) that are Christ's at His coming."

Briefly, the order of the resurrections as outlined in the bible is:

I. The Resurrection of Christ
(I Corinthians 15:20-23).

Christ is the first of the order because His resurrection constituted the first fruits which gave assurance that a great harvest was yet to come. In other words, His resurrection guarantees that all of the righteous of all ages will be raised, though at different stages. Thank God for raising Christ from the grave, which gives us the blessed assurance that we will be raised!

II. The Church Age Saints
(I Thessalonians 4:13-18; I Corinthians 15:51-58).

All believers since Acts 2 (Birthday of the church until the last one saved during this age of grace), will experience being raised to meet the Lord in the mid-air (I Thessalonians 4:13-18). Both the dead in Christ saints and the translated saints' bodies will be changed, and both groups will meet the Lord in the mid-air! This event is commonly called the Rapture – it is definitely a reunion in the sky!

III. The Old Testament Saints
(Daniel 12:2; Isaiah 26:19; Job 19:25-27

All of the righteous saints of the Old Testament (from Adam to the last saved one of the Old Testament era) will be raised to inherit the Millennium Kingdom. At that time, all of their eschatological hopes (doctrine of future events) will be realized. Thank God that time does not negate the promises God has made to the Old Testament worthies!

IV. The Two Witnesses of Revelation
(Revelation 11:1-13).
The two witnesses of this chapter will be preaching during the last of the tribulation period and experience death, but will be raised. God will miraculously summon them home – "Come up hither."

V. The Tribulation Saints
(Revelation 20:4)
Some saints of the tribulation period will experience being martyred for their faith, but they will be raised to experience the joy of entering the Millennium Kingdom. All of the righteous of all ages will be resurrected, for that group of believers is called the first resurrection or the resurrection of life (Revelation 20:6; John 5:29). All of the righteous will be raised eventually before the institution of the Millennium, with one last group remaining that will be raised after the 1,000 years (the Millennium Kingdom) is over.

VI. Resurrection of the Wicked Dead
(Revelation 20:5, 11-15; Daniel 12:2b; St. John 5:29b)

That last group is the wicked dead, from all ages. All of the wicked dead will be raised (the only general resurrection mentioned in the bible) to stand before Christ, the One presiding, and be consigned to their permanent and eternal place of abode, the lake of fire (Revelation 20:5, 11-15). Knowing about their ultimate and eternal plight, should compel us who are saved to get the gospel to them real quickly!

Bibliography
    Demaray, Donald E. Basic Beliefs. Gand Rapids: Baker Books House, 1958.
    Evangelical Training Association. Biblical Beliefs. Wheaton, Illinois: 1982.
    Evans, William. The Great Doctrines of the Bible, Chicago, Illinois: Moody Press, 1970.
    Harrison, Everett F. Baker's Dictionary of Theology: Grand Rapids, Michigan: Baker Book House, 1972.
    Ryrie, Charles C. Basic Theology. USA Canada England: Victor Books, 1986.
    Walvoord, John F. Major Bible Themes. Grand Rapids: Zondervan Publishing House, 1974.

The Grave Significance of the Lord's Supper

Matthew 26:26-30; Mark 14:22-26;
Luke 22:19-20; I Corinthians 11:23-29

The topic of the Lord's Supper is of grave importance. This event took place on the passion week of Jesus' sojourn on this earth, before He treaded up the path to Golgotha to bear the sins of the world. In fact, many of us should know that the Lord's Supper was held in conjunction with the Passover.

The Passover was a significant celebration in that, the Jews celebrated their deliverance from Egyptian bondage when the death angel passed over their homes when he saw the blood applied to the lintel of their doors; thereby, Israel's firstborn were spared (Exodus 12:12-14).

So as the Passover feast was being held, our blessed Lord inaugurates a very significant celebration by instituting the Lord's Supper. You might say that the Passover feast gave way to the Lord's Supper. According to Matthew 26:26-27, our blessed Lord took both the bread and wine, having blessed them, and gave them to His disciples, instructing them to eat and drink of it. The bread was symbolic of His body;

and the wine was symbolic of the blood of the New Covenant (Matthew 26:28). These elements did not become the actual body and blood of Christ as the doctrine of Transubstantiation teaches.

When we participate in the institution of the Lord's Supper, we should keep in mind that the elements are symbolic of the broken body and the blood of Christ that He offered for us as the paschal lamb on Calvary's cross. Our Savior served as our substitute on Calvary, dying for the sins of mankind. It was unconditional love (St. John 3:16; Romans 5:8) that prompted Him to die for guilty mankind – dying a death that He didn't deserve. He died, and was buried, but rose triumphantly from the grave (I Corinthians 15:3-4) thus, making it possible that every man might be saved if he appropriates what Christ has done for him by faith (Romans 5:1).

The Lord's Supper celebration is a special communal service that is an ordinance of the church today. It reminds us of the work that Christ wrought for us on Calvary to secure our salvation. Salvation is a free gift (St. John 10:28), but it can be appropriated only by accepting Christ's finished work on our behalf (Romans 10:9). Jesus told His disciples that He would not eat this meal again with them until the institution of His Father's Kingdom on earth

(Matthew 26:29). Jesus and His disciples sang a hymn, and left the home, and went to the Mount of Olives (Matthew 26:30).

The Lord's Supper should be taken with all known sins confessed, so that one will not be guilty of taking it in an unworthily manner. This will call for a grave self-examination (I Corinthians 11:29). Failure to discern the Lord's body, will cause one to be severely judged (I Corinthians 11:30-32).

The Seven Cross Utterances by Jesus

I. Jesus' First Cross Utterance

"Father, forgive them; for they know not what they do"
Luke 23:34

In our Lord's first cross utterance, with supreme dignity, our Lord utters words of forgiveness, not malevolence. There on that old rugged cross, He died for you and me. In this prayer from the cross, we hear Him praying, not for His own selfish interest, but for the interest of those who hated Him.

Would it have been wrong for Him to pray for Himself? No. It is never wrong for us to pray for various needs in this life, and especially when we are facing severe trials in our lives. On numerous occasions, we find many in the bible who prayed for themselves when they were undergoing perilous times. One individual that comes to mind is Peter. Being overwhelmed by the turbulent waters of the Sea of Galilee, he prayed vehemently, "Lord, save me." So it is not uncommon for people to pray for themselves; yet our Lord does not offer a prayer for His benefit, but for the benefit of others.

Noted authors have suggested that His prayer in the Greek is not just one solitary prayer, but a continuous prayer. So as His enemies were nailing Him to a cross of shame, He prayed. When they elevated the cross and placed it into its socket in the earth, He prayed. As His enemies looked upon Him in derision, He prayed.

This was not the only instance wherein our Lord prayed, for His life was one which depicted a persistent pattern of prayer. The God-man prayed not only during His crisis moments, but His life was saturated with prayer. During the beginning of His ministry to its conclusion, we find that Jesus had a firm prayer life (Luke 3:21, 5:16, 6:12, 9:28-29, 11:1, 22:41).

During His earthly ministry, our Lord engaged in performing marvelous deeds for others. He used His hands to heal others and to do a multiplication work with loaves of bread and fish, but now His hands are secured tightly to the cross. He would use His feet to run errands of mercy, but now His feet are nailed closely to an old rugged cross.

He could not summon His followers to His side, for on the cross He was beyond their reach. Being in agony and suffering a shameful and slow death, how would the Lord respond? He couldn't touch, run or move about, but He could talk – He prayed!

You will note that Jesus begins this prayer by addressing His Father. Undergoing excruciating pain, He was cognizant of the blessed relationship with which He had with His Father.

On that dismal hill of Calvary, our Lord not only was praying for others, but He was practicing what He had taught His disciples to do, namely, praying for their enemies. In the Sermon on the Mount, Jesus taught them to "Love your enemies, bless them that curse you, do good to them that hate you, and pray for them which despitefully use you, and persecute you" (Matthew 5:44).

In His prayer, the Lord went on to say that "They (His enemies) know not what they do."
He was not excusing their maltreatment of Him, but He was affirming that they didn't understand the extent of their evil in crucifying the Son of God. They were treating with extreme and supreme cruelty the very One in whom is the delight of His Father, whom vast numbers of Holy Angels worship and adore.

Lastly, Jesus was pleading with His Father to delay His judgment until they had the opportunity to repent. Was Jesus' prayer answered? Yes, on the Day of Pentecost, as Peter charged them with crucifying Christ, they were convicted and exclaimed, "Men and brethren, what shall we do?"

II. Jesus' Second Cross Utterance

"Verily I say unto thee, Today shalt thou be with me in paradise"
Luke 23:43

In Christ's first utterance from the cross (Luke 23:34), with supreme dignity and repose, our Lord uttered these words: "Father forgive them; for they know not what they do."

The scene for this utterance is still on a rugged hill outside Jerusalem, where there are three rugged crosses; the central one occupied by the most illustrious person of history, yet despised and rejected, Jesus Christ, and the other two occupied by two celebrated thieves. The enemies of our Lord thought that they were really doing something in humiliating One so majestic as Christ, placing Him between two famous criminals. Yet they were only acting out something that had been prophesied by Isaiah centuries ago, for he said in Isaiah 53:12, that, "He (Christ) was numbered with the transgressors; and He (Christ) bare the sin of many, and made intercession for the transgressors."

Even before man devised his evil scheme of placing the Son of God upon the cross, the very planning and implementation of this event was conceived in eternity past. Utilizing their most extreme cruelty, the enemies of Christ did not recognize that beyond their evil deeds, God was at work reconciling the world to Himself (2Cor. 5:19). Yes, they placed Jesus upon a humiliating and shameful cross, but the cross of Christ was essential to make possible the redemption of all men upon their belief in the only Person who is the only way to the Father, Jesus Christ (John 14:6).

While experiencing untold pain, dying in a most ignoble and shameful way, our Lord offers salvation to a repentant malefactor, evildoer, and criminal. We don't know much about this repentant malefactor, other than that he was a thief. This criminal no doubt had lived an immoral life, getting in one pursuit of trouble after another. After exhausting all of his earthly time, he was finally placed upon a cross to die as a most degrading criminal.

Now upon the cross, he could not join a local church and participate in its worship, nor could he be baptized either by immersion or by being sprinkled. He is on a cross of shame ready to enter into eternity. He had forfeited his opportunities during his earthly walk to rectify the gross mistakes of his past, and thereby become a contributing member of society. No doubt, while walking earth, he wanted to change the wrong path which he had chosen, but time had run out on him. Now he finds himself attached to a cross.

Although he and the other thief participated in the railing and reviling of Christ (Matthew 27:44), he stopped and came to a realization that he was in a hopeless and lost condition. He knew that there was something different and remarkable about the One on that central cross, for he had heard Christ pray an unusual prayer for His enemies. Now, he wanted to seize the opportunity to make aright the wrongs of his horrible past.

This criminal makes an unusual request of faith. In his request, he was not asking for relief from suffering, but the opportunity of being with Christ in His coming Kingdom. In his request, he was asking for an opportunity to be in communion with Christ, as Christ will reign supreme in the future. Christ responds by saying, "Verily I say unto thee, Today shalt thou be with me in paradise."

From the very moment the repentant thief placed his faith in Jesus Christ, Christ granted him eternal life and a place in heaven (paradise). The life of the repentant thief on the cross illustrates that anyone can be saved, if one would only come to the realization of his or her lost and hopeless condition. Having come to the realization of their condition, they need only to accept Christ's finished work on their behalf on the cross, knowing that Christ will not refuse anyone, for Christ said that, "And him that cometh to me I will in no wise cast out."

III. Jesus' Third Cross Utterance

"Woman, behold thy son!... Behold thy mother!"
John 19:26-27

The first two cross utterances of Christ (Luke 23:34, 43), recognized that our Lord was experiencing intense agony for mankind. Now at the third cross utterance, we discover that our Lord is expressing tender interest for the well-being of His mother. This same mother whom Jesus loved, was a very privileged woman, having the honor of bringing the Saviour of mankind into the world.

As she viewed her Son from the cross, she could no doubt remember the time she held and nurtured Him, probably remembering the time in which she caressed His forehead, but now He was out of her reach. She could not rub His hands or feet, for they were secured with nails to a cross of shame. From the beginning of her birth of Jesus to this moment, Mary's life was filled with sorrow. Any mother's heart would feel anguish in knowing that her first born would have to one day die for the whole world. Mary knew that the path which Christ traveled would lead Him to the cross. In fact, upon taking her baby to the temple, the aged Simeon acquainted Mary with the fact that she would experience sorrow, for he said: "Behold, this child is set for the fall and rising again of many in Israel; and for a sign which shall be spoken against' (yea, a sword shall pierce through thy own soul also,) that the thoughts of many hearts may be revealed."

Yes, Mary must have felt tremendous sorrow of heart as she witnessed the taunting voices of Jesus' enemies, and the utter disrespect shown by the Roman soldiers as they gambled at the foot of the cross. She was no doubt pondering the fact of Judas' betrayal, the desertion of Jesus' disciples, and the absence of

His four half-brothers and several sisters. Whatever the degree of her thoughts might have been, she, with quiet and serene dignity, remained loyal to her Son, even during His awful passing. From the cross, you will note that the Lord addresses His mother by the term, "woman."

We may be inclined to think that our Lord is being harsh and showing disrespect for His mother; but the term as used by the Lord is one of honor and respect. Even from the cross, our Lord was showing respect for His parent. The bible enjoins us to obey our parents (Ephesians 6:1), and certainly our Lord does that. He was so concerned for the well-being of His mother's future care until He entrusted her to someone who was so loyal, John. He did not instruct John to take her to His half-brothers and sisters, but that he would be responsible for seeing to it that Mary would be provided with love and care.

Finally, as the Lord entrusted the care of His mother to John, so has He entrusted each child of God with the responsibility of sharing His word with a spiritual deprived world. We need to declare that the same Saviour who expired on an old rugged cross, and was buried, is now alive. When anyone believes in the finished work of Christ, that person is saved, for John 3:36, says, "He that believeth on the Son hath everlasting life: and he that believeth not the Son shall not see life; but the wrath of God abideth on him."

IV. Jesus' Fourth Cross Utterance

"Eli, Eli, lama sabachthani? that is to say,
My God, my God, why hast thou forsaken me?"
A Cry of Desertion
Matthew 27:46

In the previous three cross utterances of Christ (Luke 23:34, 43; John 19:26-27), Christ experienced untold and unusual agony as the God-man. In verse 46 of Matthew 27, out of the midst of stark darkness, we find our Lord uttering a cry of being forsaken, for He said, "My God, my God, why hast thou forsaken me?" The word forsaken as defined by Webster means – "to leave, abandon, desert." I can't think of a more tragic word than the word "forsaken." I am thinking of a child whose love for its mother transcends life, only to find out that mother's life has been cut short by a fatal car accident, with the child not being able to see mother again. Not being able to see mother again, that child will feel the chilling effect of being abandoned. To be forsaken by anyone is hurtful, yet it is a part of life.

Two questions come to mind from this verse: "Can anyone measure the intense depths of this cry and "why" did Jesus cry out of darkness?" Answering the first question, this cry of Jesus is intensely deeper than any ocean or river. Although His cry of desertion is immeasurable, it is for certain that it is not one of defeat, for Jesus was very conscious of His surroundings. He was not crying out of a sense of despair, but because He felt the full penalty of being forsaken by the Father.

The second part of the question can be answered in terms of viewing darkness as a symbol of the heinous nature of sin. Our Lord was crucified according to Mark 15:25 during the third hour (9:00a.m.). From the third hour until the sixth hour (9:00 a.m.- noon), Jesus was suffering at the hands of man. The Calvary scene depicts not only the depth of God's love for us, but it details the enormous hatred of man toward its creator. The co-creator of this universe, Jesus Christ, yields in supreme dignity to the awfulness of man's extreme hatred of Him, and dies in ignominy and unusual shame; yet, He was in total possession of Himself. And now in supreme repose, He is experiencing the bitter cup of being alone and forsaken by His Father.

During the last three hours of being on the cross, from the sixth until the ninth hour (noon – 3:00 p.m.), we find our Lord suffering at the hands of God. It was during the last three hours on the cross that Our Lord was serving as our substitute and representative as the sacrifice for sin. The last three hours upon that cross must have been awfully painstaking for Christ, in the sense that, as our substitute, and sin-bearer, He was forsaken by His Father because God could not look upon sin. I am thankful that Jesus died, for there was no one available to pay fully and sufficiently the awful penalty for sin. The sinless one died in our stead. Who can really ascertain the depth of meaning involved in verse 45? Although its meaning cannot be measured, it nevertheless displayed the love that God had for us, and the extreme hatred man had toward Him.

If you accept Christ's finished work on Calvary and His resultant burial and resurrection, you can experience salvation, for John 5:24 says: "Verily, verily, I say unto you, He that heareth my word, and believeth on Him that sent me, hath everlasting life, and shall not come into condemnation; but is passed from death unto life."

V. Jesus' Fifth Cross Utterance

"I Thirst"
An Acknowledgment of a Need
John 19:28

Noting the previous cross sayings of Christ (Luke 23:34, 43; John 19:26-27; Matthew 27:46), we now come to the fifth cross utterance of Christ. As our sinless substitute on the cross, where He has undergone tremendous pain and ridicule, we hear Him expressing a need – "I thirst." Christ was so preoccupied with His mission of dying for the sins of the world; and while on the cross, He never sought any pity from anyone, nor did He express any physical need of Himself. But now, we find Him acknowledging a physical need – "I thirst."

The Lord had a right to be thirsty, for His body was suspended between heaven and earth, and His blood was draining, which would cause anybody to elicit a need for water. The last recorded time that He drank was probably during the Passover meal He had with His beloved disciples. You must understand that He had been on the cross for approximately six hours; and in view of everything that transpired after He was betrayed by Judas in the Garden of Gethsemane to His mocked trials, He was very exhausted, and indeed, He needed some water. Imagine if you please, the co-creator of this vast universe, eliciting a need for a drink!

His acknowledgment serves to prove that He was perfect man (sinless), yet as God, He owns everything, including water. As perfect man, He experienced being limited, in that, He experiences all of the limitations of being a man, yet without sin. As a perfect man, He became tired, weary, and He even wept and slept. But as God, He could command a friend to come forth from the grave, and even rebuke a raging sea and wind to behave and come to calmness. Yet, our Lord subjected Himself to the limitations of being a man in order to die in our stead for the salvation of all men.

Christ knew very well the work of redemption that He was ordained in eternity past to accomplish, and that He must bear the full impact of the weight and awfulness of sin. He was not going to complain nor elicit any sympathy from mortal man, but merely acknowledge a need – "I thirst." The world responded to Jesus' need of a drink this way, in that, Matthew 27:34 says, "They gave Him vinegar to drink mingled with gall: and when He had tasted thereof, He would not drink." They gave Him a drink which would help to ease His pain, but He refused to drink it. Our Lord bore the full measure of the tremendous weight of sin for all of Adam's lost posterity.

I am thankful that He died for lost humanity, and now He welcomes all to drink of Him spiritually, and truly your soul's thirst will be satisfied. Jesus Christ is the only one who can satisfy the soul's thirst, for John 4:14 says, "But whosoever drinketh of the water that I shall give him shall never thirst; but the water that I shall give him shall be in him a well of water springing up into everlasting life."

VI. Jesus' Sixth Cross Utterance

"It is finished"
A Proclamation of Triumph
John 19:30

Acknowledging the previous cross utterances of Christ (Luke 23:34; 43; John 19:26-27; Matthew 27:46; John 19:28), we come now to Christ's six utterance from the cross. At the outset of reading this message of victory proclaimed by our Lord, a poignant thought invaded my mind and I asked myself the following questions: "Did not God create man, the apex of His creation, on the sixth day, and isn't this proclamation of Jesus the sixth of His cross utterances?" In the bible, six is the number for man because he was created on the sixth day. Furthermore, it seems rather striking that our Lord will enunciate an exclamation of complete victory as He speaks from the cross, announcing during His sixth cross utterance that the very work for which He came in time to fulfill, was now being fulfilled.

As stated previously, Jesus was well acquainted with the purpose for His earthly mission, and with every passion of His being, He was absolutely focused in His drive to be man's substitute for sin. Nothing in His whole creation, or nobody in it, could deter Christ from fulfilling His mission of dying as man's expiatory sacrifice. So, from start to finish, our Lord's life was bent toward Calvary. Although having achieved much fame as a master teacher, preacher, and a miraculous healer, Calvary was always on His mind, for I can hear Him as He said in Mark 10:45, that, "For even the Son of man came not to be ministered unto, but to minister, and to give His life a ransom for many." On that rugged cross, and as man's expiatory sacrifice for sin, our Lord pungently suffered and met all of the demands of God's righteousness, paying in full the penalty for sin.

When our Lord knew that His work of redemption, which was conceived and initiated in eternity past, was completed, He expired in dignity, never again to experience the shame and disgrace of being treated so unjustly by the vicious deeds of man. In Jesus' statement – "It is finished," what did He have reference to? Certainly, all of the ignominy and shame associated with being man's expiatory sacrifice for sin, was now complete. Jesus will not have to experience being betrayed by Judas, or even experience being tried six times in courts of injustice, not being mocked and derided by unfriendly and wicked onlookers as He hung from a cross of shame, as He suffered supremely for man.

Moreover, His sixth proclamation suggests that the prophecy regarding His birth, life, death, and resurrection was fulfilled. It should bring assurance to our faith that the prophecy pertaining to our Lord's first advent into the world has been absolutely and utterly fulfilled. And we can be completely assured that all of the prophecies regarding His second coming will be fulfilled. As I conclude, there is yet an ultimate reason or purpose for Jesus making this proclamation of triumph. When Christ said, "It is finished" (tete, lestai), He was disclosing or revealing that all of the sacrifices made in Old Testament found its fulfillment in Him. All of the sacrifices made in the Old Testament could never take away sin; it merely covered the sins. But Jesus in His death, completely took away sin. No wonder John the Baptist testified and said, "Behold the Lamb of God, which taketh away the sin of the world."

VII. Jesus' Seventh Cross Utterance

"Father, into thy hands I commend my spirit"
In the Father's Hands
Luke 23:46

There were previously six cross utterances of Christ (Luke 23:34, 43; John 19:26-27; Matthew 27:46; John 19:28, 30), now we have arrived at His final spoken word from the cross. The last cross expression serves as a fitting climax to the wonderful and fruitful ministry of our Saviour. Our Lord was so preoccupied with fulfilling His Father's will until He wasn't going to let anything or anybody deter Him from finishing the work of redemption to which He came to complete, for I can hear Him as He said, "For the Son of man is come to seek and to save that which was lost" (Luke 19:10). Jesus came to die for sinful humanity and to work a great redemption for man.

Having announced with a great exuberance of victory in His sixth cross saying, "It is finished," meaning that all of the sacrifices in the Old Testament period found their completion in Him, we come now to His last cross expression as found in Luke 23:46, which says, "And when Jesus had cried with a loud voice, He said, "Father, into thy hands I commend my spirit: and having said thus, He gave up the ghost." He announced these words after He had met the full demands of God's infinite justice, for God's justice and the full demands of His righteousness, required the death of Jesus Christ. There was no other way by which God was going to be appeased or satisfied, save only the death of Christ. So when Jesus had completely met the demands of God's justice and righteousness, He was now ready to fall into the loving and infinite hands of His Father.

The separation that existed when Jesus became our sin-bearer as He cried out "My God, My God, why hast thou forsaken me?", has now been restored, and now His work of redemption has been completed. You will note that His last saying was His seventh which was very important to Jewish reckoning. The number seven means perfection.

Thus, man was created on the sixth day and on the seventh God rested, not because He was tired, but because His work of creation was complete. Now, in a comparable way, we find that Christ had announced, "It is finished," during His sixth cross utterance only to exclaim now that His work of redemption for man was complete, He could expire into the awesome and loving hands of His Father. When one commends oneself to the Father, he is safe and secured.

When one commends oneself to the Father, he is totally entrusting one's life to His safekeeping. These words of Jesus, "Father into thy hands I commend my spirit," disclose or reveal that Jesus' life was ordered or was in complete communion with Him. Having gone through the ordeal of suffering tremendously for man, He was now ready to offer His life into the safe haven of His Father's hands. Jesus, who had suffered at the hands of man, having been treated unjustly by them, was now ready to go home. Well, when your work is over, and you have done all that has been exacted upon you by the Father, you can commit your life to the safekeeping of God. Jesus will now have to go through the ordeal of being betrayed by Judas, or even being arrested in a garden, and being tried six times in unjust courts, or of experiencing being spat upon and beaten unmercifully as the Son of man, as He toiled up a hill for you and me.

He died in a most ignominious fashion, but let me submit to you that He surrendered to the maltreatment of man. He ordered the time in which He would submit to the cruel hands of man, and He ordered the time in which He would die. Jesus decided the exact moment in which He would die, for He voluntarily gave up His life. And when His life's mission was complete, He lovingly submitted His life to the care of God.

Then when your work is over, you can go home and experience uninterrupted fellowship with God. In the "Father's hands" there is safety, security and stability. When you are in the "Father's hand's you are eternally saved, and you need not fear about the prospect of spending an eternity apart from Him (hell), for Jesus said, "And I give unto them eternal life; and they shall never perish, neither shall any may pluck them out of my hand. My Father, which gave them me, is greater that all; and no man is able to pluck them out of my Father's hand. I and my Father are one." (John 10:28-30).

Thank God, that through faith in His Son's finished work, one can fall into the safety of the Father's hands, never to worry about the peril of going to hell, for Acts 4:12, says, "Neither is there salvation in any other: for there is none other name under heaven given among men, whereby we must be saved."

Matthew

Matthew, the author of this book, is also referred to as "Levi", the son of Alpheus (Mark 2:14, Luke 5:27). Moreover, Levi was a despised and hated tax collector who worked for the Roman government; thus he was looked upon in a degrading manner among the Jews who resented the Roman's control over them. However, Levi (Matthew) responded unhesitatingly to the Master's call to follow Him and influenced other publicans and sinners to listen to the life changing words of the Master teacher, Jesus Christ (Mark 2:14-15, Luke 5:27-29). That fact alone leads to this admonition, "When we have had a life changing experience with the Master, we should invite and influence others to experience the same by presenting the claims of the Gospel to them."

Matthew's purpose in writing this gospel is to present "Christ as King." Matthew presents many quotations from the Old Testament to confirm Jesus' claims that He is the long-awaited Messiah (the Anointed One). At the very outset of his presentation, Matthew shows that Jesus is the Messiah by tracing His genealogy back to Abraham and showing that Christ is a direct descendant of David to establish that He is the "King of the Jews."

The splendid ministry of the King of Israel is marvelously presented by Matthew's presentation of the King's credentials – expressed through His authoritative words, teachings, and His mighty deeds as Miracles. His teaching ministry consisted in His discourses mentioned in this book, namely: the Sermon on the Mount (Chapters 5-7); the Parables (Chapter 13); the Olivet Discourse (Chapters 24-25).

After the King had been duly introduced and His credentials presented, the Jews, for the most part, reject His claims and works, which leads to His arrest, trials and crucifixion (Matthew Chapter 26-27). But the blessed King of Israel, Jesus Christ, authenticated His claim that He is the Son of God, the long awaited King of Israel, by rising from the dead (Matthew 28).

If any unsaved man places his faith in Jesus Christ he can be saved, for Christ said, "All that the Father giveth me shall come to me; and him that cometh to me I will in no wise cast out" (St. John 6:37).

The book of Matthew may be outlined as follows:

I. The Introduction to the King. Chapters 1:1-4:11
II. The Grand Teachings of the King. Chapters 4:12-7:29

III. The Grand Presentation, Power and Rejection of the King. Chapters 8:1-27:66

IV. The Mighty Triumph of the King. Chapter 28:1-20.

Mark

The briefest account of the magnificent life of Christ, the book of Mark was written by John Mark, a cousin of Barnabas (Colossians 4:10). Mark gives a concise portrayal of the exciting ministry of the "Perfect Servant" as He preaches, teaches, and heals the masses of people. In addition, Mark depicts the life of Christ acting in a servant role of ministry to others, with that ministry culminating on a rugged cross of shame as He gives His life a ransom for many (Mark 10:45).

Without much dispute, many scholars agree that Mark is the author of this grand gospel. He was not chosen as one of Jesus' twelve disciples; however, being in close association with Peter, Mark was granted much authority to this marvelous gospel, for Peter became Mark's chief source of information.

The probable date of this gospel was between A.D. 55-65. Many scholars agree that the book of Mark was written sometime before the destruction of the temple because Mark mentions a prophecy of the temple's destruction in Mark 13:2.

The aim of Mark's gospel is to present Christ as the Servant of Jehovah actively going about doing the will of the Father. The key verse of this book is found in Mark 10:45, "For even the Son of man came not to be ministered unto, but to minister, and to give His life a ransom for many."

The expression, "a ransom for many," conveys the idea that our blessed Lord sacrificed His life for all mankind. A verse that also captures the fact that Christ died as a substitute for all mankind is found in II Corinthians 5:21, "For He hath made Him to be sin for us, who knew no sin; that we might be made the righteousness of God in Him."

God the Father gave Christ, the sinless Lamb of God, as a voluntary offering for the sins of mankind; and Christ died a shameful death, paying fully the penalty for sin. In Mark's gospel, Christ's ministry of three and a half years of teaching, preaching and healing will result in utter rejection from the chief priests, scribes and elders. Christ's ministry of compassion for the physical and spiritual needs of others resulted in Him being arrested, placed on trial, and crucified.

But the same seemingly defeated servant will rise triumphantly from the dead (Mark 16). The grand resurrection of Christ was God's validation that the death of Christ fully satisfied God's wrath against sin.

This book of Mark can be outlined briefly this way:

I. The Person of Christ in Service to Others. Chapters 1-10.
II. The Person of Christ Sacrificing for Others. Chapters 11-16.
The brilliant career of ministry or our blessed Lord can be summed up in two words – "service" and "sacrifice."

Luke

In this Gospel, Dr. Luke, a Gentile writer and physician, writes from the viewpoint of presenting Christ as the "ideal perfect man." He instructs us in this gospel that truly the "Son of God" became the perfect "Son of man". In essence, Jesus Christ came from heaven above to dwell among us in an effort to save lost humanity. The "lofty One" came to rescue the capstone of His creation, man, from the doom and gloom of sin. Every man born after the likeness of

Adam is in dire need of a Saviour, one who will totally satisfy God's total demand against sin. Jesus Christ sufficiently satisfied God's demand against sin by dying a vicarious death for mankind. Christ's sacrifice thus made it possible for man to have a proper or fitting standing before Holy God by faith in His shed blood (Romans 5:1).

With reference to the gospel of Luke, this writer gives a portrait of Jesus' ancestry, birth and early life before he presents the mighty words and deeds of the Son of man as He ministers to mankind. Dr. Luke was not an apostle of Jesus Christ as Matthew or the Apostle John, but he relied heavily on the testimony of eye witnesses in gathering his information. Thus, he was able to gather the information needed to supply his readers with a comprehensive and carefully arranged historical analysis of the ministry of our blessed Lord – presenting to us the fact that Jesus had a three-fold ministry of preaching, teaching and healing (St. Matthew 4:23).

Dr. Luke unfolds Jesus' claims and mighty deeds (miracles) in order to show that Jesus Christ is truly the Son of God, who came to seek and to save mankind from the depths of sin and despair. The key verse of this powerful gospel account is found in St.

Luke 19:10, "For the Son of man is come to seek and to save that which was lost."

Some of the most interesting teachings of the Bible are found in the book of Luke such as: The Story of the Good Samaritan, The Prodigal Son, The Account of Zaccheus being saved, Jesus' encounter with the sisters of Bethany, Mary and Martha, and Jesus' conversation with the two disciples on the road of Emmaus.

Dr. Luke unfolds to us that those who believe Christ's claims are challenged to estimate the genuine essence of what discipleship really means. In contrast, those who reject His claims do so through their unbelief, and the highest exhibition of their unbelief was evident in the world placing Jesus on a cross of shame. Thus, Christ's ministry of compassion ended in utter shame. He died as mankind's perfect sacrifice for sin, coming from the lofty heights of heaven to expiate and pay sufficiently mankind's full debt of sin. But this same Jesus that died on Friday dismally, was raised from the grave triumphantly on Sunday morning, ensuring that God the Father was totally and completely satisfied with the work Christ wrought for us on Calvary. His resurrection guaranteed that Christ's work of compassion in evangelism will be advanced through His apostles as they will be equipped through the potent power of the Holy Spirit.

The gospel of Luke may be outlined this way:

I. The Son of Man Introduced or Presented - Chapters 1:1-4:13 (A presentation of His ancestry, birth and early development.)
II. The Ministry and Rejection of the Son of Man - Chapters 4:14-19:27 (A presentation of His mighty claims and deeds, culminating in His rejection.)
III. The Son of Man Crucified and Raised from the Dead – Chapters 19:28-24:53 (A presentation of His crucifixion and resurrection and exaltation.)

John

The Gospel of John differs slightly from the Synoptic Gospels (Matthew, Mark and Luke) in that it records events and discourses not found in the first three Gospel accounts. Moreover, the Apostle John, a member of the inner circle of disciples of Jesus (Peter, James and John himself), writes to prove unmistakably that Jesus Christ is God in the flesh, who came from heaven on a mission of mercy to rescue mankind by dying in his stead as a sinless substitute for sin (Mark 10:45; St. John 1:29). Thus, the "Eternal Word," the "Son of God," became the "Son of Man," who was born in order to save mankind. It can be said that "we (mankind) were born in order to live; Christ was born in order to die."

In addition, this Gospel unfolds, like the Synoptic Gospels, that Jesus Christ is truly unique in the following ways: (1) the manner in which He was born, for He was virgin born, (2) the manner in which He spoke for He spoke as One having authority, (3) the power by which He ministered, He displayed power in several realms, over nature, disease, demons and death, and (4) the way in which He died, He voluntarily gave His life as a substitute for mankind.

The aim of the Apostle John's presentation is to set forth Jesus Christ as "Deity", fully God, in order to evoke in His readers believing faith, the faith so essential to gain eternal life. The author of this Gospel is portrayed as the "one whom Jesus loved" (St. John 13:23; 20:2; 21:7, 20).

The central purpose or theme of the Gospel of John is found in St. John 20:30-31, "Any many other signs truly did Jesus in the presence of His disciples, which are not written in this book: But these are written, that ye might believe that Jesus is the Christ, the Son of God; and that believing ye might have life through His name."

The Apostle John presents clearly Christ's matchless claims, His Seven "I AM Statements recorded in St. John 6:35, 8:12, 10:9, 10:11, 11:25, 14:6, 15:1 and other claims. His unusual deeds, His miracles are presented in St. John 2:1-11, 4:43-54, 5:1-9, 6:1-13, 6:15-21, 9:1-7, 11:1-44, 21:1-14. His claims and deeds were presented to prove that Jesus Christ is God in the flesh. In conclusion, this Gospel unfolds that there were two responses to Christ's claims and His deeds – belief and unbelief. To those who believed, they were granted eternal life (St. John 1:12) and to those who rejected Him, remained in their sins (St. John 8:24).

The climactic proof that Jesus is the Son of God was demonstrated in His victorious resurrection from the grave. And because He rose from the grave, all believers have the guarantee that we will be raised to spend eternity with God.

Acts

The book of Acts connects the Gospels and the Epistles, serving as a bridge between the life of Jesus and the beginning of the Church. This book was written by Dr. Luke around A.D. 62. Dr. Luke is tracing the progress of the Great Commission, a commission initiated from the lips of our triumphant Saviour before He was elevated to His familiar home, heaven (St. Luke 24:49-53; Matthew 28:19-20).

Acts is a continuation of Dr. Luke's account in the Gospel of Luke. Acts deals with the progressive growth of the church that starts in Jerusalem (Chapters 1-7), promotes through persecution in Judea and Samaria (Chapters 8-12), and extends unto the uttermost in Chapters 13-28. Thus, the book of Acts supplies the historical growth of Christianity for thirty years. Without this contribution from the compiled treatise of Dr. Luke, we would be void of any historical background for an understanding of the Epistles.

The key verse of this book is Acts 1:8, which says, "But ye shall receive power after that the Holy Spirit is come upon you: and ye shall be witnesses unto me both in Jerusalem, and in all Judea, and in Samaria, and unto the uttermost part of the earth."

The book of Acts records the bold witness of the once fearful disciples, once they had been endowed with the blessed promise of the Holy Spirit (Luke 24:49).

The disciples were endowed with the promise of the Holy Spirit on the Day of Pentecost as He equipped them for service.

In Chapters 1-7, we are confronted with the bold witness of Peter, the leading spokesman for the Jerusalem church. Peter stood up boldly and preached Jesus to his audience and the "word" brought conviction to the hearts of three thousand souls – and they were saved (Acts 2:41). But the mighty message of Christ crucified and raised from the dead was only shared in the environs of Jerusalem.

With the aid of persecution, the Gospel will invade the areas of Judea and Samaria (Chapters 8-12), with Stephen and Phillip, serving as the historical spokesmen and links between Peter and Paul. After Stephen's defense before the Sanhedrin and his home-going after he was stoned to death for declaring the truth, we are introduced to a persecuting but transformed proponent of the Gospel, the Apostle Paul (Chapters 13-28).

The Apostle Paul was dramatically transformed on the road to Damascus, and his Damascus experience had an impressionable impact upon his witness, for he will rehearse that experience of Acts 9:1-18, on two other occasions (Acts 22:1-21; Acts 26:12-18).

After the church's expansion in Chapters 8-12, Dr. Luke will focus on the three missionary journeys and the three trials of the Apostle Paul (Chapters 13-28). This book concludes with Paul being under house arrest for two years (Acts 28:30). Many writers agree that during this time frame of two years, Paul wrote four prison Epistles – Ephesians, Philippians, Colossians and Philemon.

Romans

The book of Romans is one of the most inspiring works in the New Testament. It was written about A.D. 57, as Paul came to the end of his third missionary journey (Acts 18:23-21:14; Romans 15:19). Many scholars believe that Paul penned this epistle during his three-month stay in Corinth.

In this epistle, Paul presents a brilliant masterpiece of God's plan of salvation, a salvation conceived in eternity past, but carried out in time through the sacrificial offering of Jesus Christ as man's substitute on Calvary. Through faith in God's gift of salvation, Jesus Christ, mankind can be "Justified freely by

God's grace through redemption that is in Christ Jesus" (Romans 3:24).

After Paul's brief introduction of this epistle (1:1-17), Paul delves into his intriguing argument dealing with the fact that both Jews and Gentiles had a need for God's righteousness through Christ; and that both Jews and Gentiles were guilty because they came short of reaching God's holy standard (1:18-3:20). The Gentiles were guilty because they suppressed the truth of the knowledge of God they received from natural creation and their conscience (1:18-32). The Jews were guilty because they had the law but didn't live up to its holy standard. Paul concluded that both groups were condemned: "all have sinned and come short of the glory of God" (Romans 3:23).

However, in Romans 3:21-5:21, Paul will show unequivocally that mankind is justified, that is declared righteous, only through the sacrificial offering of Jesus Christ through faith. When mankind places his faith in Christ's finished work of Calvary, he is fully justified and "declared not guilty."

Paul will declare that the good news of the Gospel is centered around and in Jesus Christ and that a life of righteousness is exacted upon those who believe (6:1-8:39). Therefore, Paul will begin his section on sanctification (6:1-8:39), and he will explain that holiness is required by the believer.

In the next section (Chapters 9-11), Paul deals with the issue of Israel in the plan of God. He explains that Israel was elected by God (9:1-9:29), but presently, she has been set aside by God because of unbelief (9:30-10:21). However, in the future, Israel will be restored (11:1-11:36).

In the first eleven chapters of this book, Paul discussed the doctrinal basis for believers' righteous standing before God (1:1-11:36), now in Chapters 12-16, he will unfold the practical righteousness expected in their daily lives as a result of their salvation.

In conclusion, salvation is a plan conceived by God which starts and ends with Him, and that He has included us, the believers, as a part of that plan.

I Corinthians

It has been said by many noted scholars that the word "Corinth" is synonymous with infamy and wickedness. Corinth was a prominent commercial center located in Southern Greece. This city was famous for its immorality and pagan practices.

In the midst of a city noted for its wickedness, the Apostle Paul came with the gospel message and established a church during his second missionary campaign (Acts 18:1-7). Although a church was established in Corinth, Paul had an awesome task of "keeping Corinth out of a growing church."

This church was plagued with such problems as the report of incest among family members (Chapter 5:1-13), legal issues among believers (Chapter 6:1-11), and other sexual immorality discussed (Chapter 6:12-20). Coupled with these issues, Paul will also address such crucial matters as: marriage (Chapter 7), things offered to idols (Chapter 8-11), public worship (Chapters 11-14), the resurrection (Chapter 15), and concerns for the collection for the poor saints in Jerusalem (Chapter 16).

A key verse of this epistle is found in I Corinthians 6:19-20, which says, "What? Know ye not that your body is the temple of the Holy Ghost which is in you, which ye have of God, and ye are not your own?"

One of the most beloved Chapters in all of the bible is found in I Corinthians Chapter 13, "Though I speak with the tongues of men and of angels, and have not charity, I am become as sounding brass, or a tinkling cymbal." This beloved Chapter gives one of the highest expressions of how genuine love manifests itself. Lastly, the Apostle Paul gives a staunch defense of the doctrine of the Resurrection, a doctrine that is the bedrock of our Christian faith and hope. Without the verity of the historical resurrection of Jesus Christ, believers have no basis for believing that they will rise again and live eternally with their bridegroom, Jesus Christ. But because Christ lives, believers will live also (St. John 14:19). The book of I Corinthians may be outlined as follows:

I. The Problem of the Church – Division
(I Corinthians Chapters 1:1-4:21)
II. The Plague of the Church – Defections
(I Corinthians Chapters 5:1—6:20)
III. The Perplexities of the Church – Difficulties
(I Corinthians Chapters 7-16:24)

II Corinthians

In this second epistle, Paul is presenting a staunch defense of his Apostolic authority. He vindicates his authority as an apostle of Jesus Christ, because the Judaizers attacked the character, conduct and the calling of Apostle Paul. They claimed that Paul ministered with the wrong motives. What a vigorous attack on a person who served with pure motives!

Our ministries will be attacked by various people. With that thought in mind, it would behoove us to walk circumspectly in this dismal world and to heed to Christ's command to – "Let your light so shine before men, that they may see your good works, and glorify your Father which is in heaven" (Matthew 5:16).

This epistle was written by the Apostle Paul while he was in Macedonia in A.D. 56. This book contains, not only a staunch defense of his apostolic authority, but reveals such doctrines as: the Christian's outlook in suffering for Christ (II Corinthians 4:8-18); the Resurrection and the Judgment Seat of Christ (Bema) (II Corinthians 5:1-13); the ministry of reconciliation (II Corinthians 5:14-21); and the biblical perspective on giving (II Corinthians Chapters 8-9).

As it relates to a believer's salvation, this epistle reveals that Christ is our substitute (II Corinthians 5:21), and that the Holy Spirit has sealed us (II Corinthians 1:22). After defending the basis of his calling, message, character and conduct as a servant of Christ, Paul gives to us God's plan as it relates to the right way to give. He concludes that section in Chapters 8-9 by demonstrating that Christ is the Supreme model in giving, for II Corinthians 9:15, says, "Thanks be unto God for His unspeakable gift."

The key verses of this epistle are found in II Corinthians 4:5-6 and 5:17-19, which state: "For we preach not ourselves, but Christ Jesus the Lord; and ourselves your servants for Jesus' sake. For God, who commanded the light to shine out of darkness, hath shined in our hearts, to give the light of the knowledge of the glory of God in the face of Jesus Christ." "Therefore if any man be in Christ, he is a new creature: old things are passed away; behold, all things are become new. And all things are of God, who hath reconciled us to Himself by Jesus Christ, and hath given to us the ministry of reconciliation; To wit, that God was in Christ, reconciling the world unto Himself, not imputing their trespasses unto them; and hath committed unto us the word of reconciliation."

In the last section of the book (Chapters 10-13), Paul vindicates his apostleship by showing that he has the spiritual credentials to serve as an apostle. The book of II Corinthians may be outlined as follows:

I. Paul's Defense of His Ministry (Chapters 1-7)
II. Paul's Declaration on God's Plan for Christian Giving (Chapters 8-9)
III. Paul's Defense of His Apostolic Credentials (Chapters 10-13)

Galatians

The book of Galatians proclaims that we have been justified by means of total faith in Jesus Christ apart from any degree of works. We have been set free by believing in Christ's finished work on Calvary; thus, the gospel is all about what Christ has done for us. Belief in His finished work on our behalf has resulted in perfect liberty and the resultant power to live aright for Him through the agency of the indwelling Holy Spirit.

The theme of Galatians is "Justification by faith apart from the works of the law (Galatians 2:16). In Chapters 1-2, Paul will defend his apostolic authority, and in doing so, will confirm the gospel message of God's grace. In Chapters 3-4, Paul will unfold a firm defense of the principle of justification by faith to counteract the Judaizers false gospel of works. Lastly, in Chapters 5-6, Paul will show that Christian liberty is not a license to sin even though one has been liberated from the bondage of the law.

The justification, the act of being "declared righteous", we possess in Christ Jesus produces Christian liberty; however, it is not liberty that gives us the license to sin. Granted that we are "saints who sin," but we should not be complacent in our sin habits. Moreover, sinning should conscientiously affect us to the point that we confess our sins (I John 1:9).

In this epistle, Paul is giving a staunch defense of the gospel of grace by vigorously showing that he possesses the credentials as an apostle of Jesus Christ. He is also vigorously attacking the Judaizers for propagating a false gospel of works. The Galatian believers were guilty of, and even being contented in, leaving the gospel of faith and following in the path of the gospel of works.

The path that the Galatians were following greatly troubled Paul. Thus, Paul will reveal to us that a man is justified wholly by faith in Christ Jesus apart from any works of the law. Paul will prove in this book that the purpose of the law was to bring men to Christ; moreover, the law served to reveal the sinfulness of man, not to save man. Only Christ Jesus has the power to emancipate mankind from the shackles of sin through belief in His finished work. As believers, we have been indwelt by the Holy Spirit at the moment of Salvation (I Corinthians 6:19), and that we should surrender to the Holy Spirit in our daily walk. Thus, in order to walk correctly as children of God, we need to walk by means of Him who indwells, for Galatians 5:16, says, "This I say then, walk in the Spirit, and ye shall not fulfill the lust of the flesh." The book of Galatians may be outlined as follows:

I. Paul's Defense of His Apostolic Authority (Galatians 1:1-2:21)
II. Paul's Presentation of the Principle of Justification is by Faith Apart from the Law (Galatians 3:1-4:31)
III. Fruit of Being Justified by Faith – A Believers Walk (Galatians 5:1-6:18)

Ephesians

The book of Ephesians was written around A.D. 60-61. This book is included in Paul's Prison Epistle Section – Ephesians, Philippians, Colossians, and Philemon.

Paul's labor in this commercial center of Asia Minor was certainly productive, with the gospel being propagated throughout the province. After a long stay of three years, Paul's effective ministry in Ephesus was met with opposition, for a severe uproar occurred in the Ephesian theater. Paul was forced to move on to Macedonia. However, Paul did get an opportunity to say farewell to the Ephesian elders before going to Jerusalem (Acts 20:17-38).

In reading the Pauline epistles, and the book of Acts, it is evident that Paul was determined to allow nothing to prevent him from preaching God's inspired word. He didn't allow any circumstance or anybody to deter him from preaching the gospel.

Once he received his directives from God on that road to Damascus, he was resigned to do God's will. He was resolved to preach God's unsearchable riches without reservation, for he said – "For I have not shunned to declare unto you all the counsel of God" (Acts 20:27).

The theme of this epistle is the wealthy position of the believers, and because of that position, the expected practice of their Christian walk. The practical walk of a Christian must always be based on his wealthy position in Christ Jesus. Paul was careful in writing this epistle stressing that the believers will come to apprehend their spiritual calling so that they might understand their expected conduct.

The key verses of this epistle are found in Ephesians 2:8-10 and 4:1, and they read: "For by grace are ye saved through faith; and that not of yourselves: it is the gift of God: Not of works, lest any man should boast. For we are His workmanship, created in Christ Jesus unto good works, which God hath before ordained that we should walk in them." "I therefore, the prisoner of the Lord, beseech you that ye walk worthy of the vocation wherewith ye are called." The epistle of Ephesians may be outlined this way:

I. The Elevated Position of the Believers (Wealth) 1:1-3:21
II. The Expected Practice of the Believers (Walk) 4:1-6:24

Philippians

The book of Philippians is one of Paul's prison epistles, along with Ephesians, Colossians and Philemon. In this warm and embracing epistle, Paul is expressing his untold gratitude for a church that supported him financially while he was imprisoned in

Rome during his first imprisonment. This epistle was probably written in A.D. 62.

In this book, Paul also seeks to encourage and edify the faith of all saints even in the midst of adverse circumstances. No matter what trials one may be undergoing, this book has a very definite message for a believer – "through the power of Christ, one can rise above adverse circumstances."

Even in the midst of Paul being incarcerated, he explodes with confidence in Christ Jesus, and with the power of Christ, he was able to meet the challenges of the ministry with joy. In fact, Paul uses the word "joy" or "rejoice" in this epistle some sixteen times. In conveying the theme of this book, Paul expresses his love and gratitude for the believers at Philippi and to also exhorts them to a lifestyle of unity, holiness, and joy.

The key verses of this book are found in Philippians 1:21 and 4:12 and they read, "For to me to live is Christ, and to die is gain." "I know both how to be abased, and I know how to abound: everywhere and in all things I am instructed both to be full and to be hungry, both to abound and to suffer need."

Paul's whole existence was centered in Christ, and when a believer's whole life is centered with Christ's thoughts and actions, he will live a life of contentment. To the apostle Paul, Christ meant everything: in Chapter 1, Christ was his whole existence (1:21); in Chapter 2, Christ was the manifestation and model of genuine humility (2:5); in Chapter 3, Christ is the source who will transform a believer's body of humiliation that it may be conformed to His glorious body (3:21); and in Chapter 4, Christ is the source of Paul's power over circumstances (4:13).

In closing, the key to having a successful existence while undergoing various trials in this life, is to center one's thoughts and actions in Jesus Christ, for in doing so, one will rise above the adverse circumstances of life.

Colossians

Colossians is another Pauline Epistle that exalts Christ as the "Head of the Church." This book was written while Paul was incarcerated in Rome during his first imprisonment in A.D. 60 or 61. We call the following Epistles (Ephesians, Philippians,

Colossians, Philemon) prison epistles because they were written while Paul was imprisoned in Rome.

The church at Colossae was founded by Epaphras (1:4-8; 2:1), who was converted under Paul's ministry during Paul's third missionary journey in which Paul was engaged in a three year ministry in Ephesus. In this epistle, Paul's aim was to exalt the person and work of Christ. During His incarnation, Christ left the lofty heights of heaven to dwell among sinful mankind. Serving as man's substitute on a rugged cross of Calvary, He provided the sufficient sacrifice to expiate man's sin.

Through faith in Christ's sufficient work on Calvary, mankind can be completely justified (Romans 5:1). Through faith in His work alone, mankind can be completely exonerated from the guilt of sin. This epistle informs us that Christ is preeminent and completely sufficient for any spiritual and practical need of the believer. Because of the exalted Person and work of Christ, the believer has all the power necessary to live the Christian life aright. We need not live defeated lives, because in Christ, we have the sufficiency necessary to live transformed lives.

The basic theme of this epistle is the preeminence and sufficiency of the person and work of Christ. There is no reason for believers to engage in ritualism, mysticism, asceticism and speculation, when they have all that they need in Christ. The strange heresy that existed in this predominantly-Gentile church was a threatening one, and Paul sought to combat that heresy by exalting the person and work of Christ, showing that a believer is completely sufficient in Him.

The key verses of this epistle are found in Colossians 2:9-10 and chapters 3:1-2, and they read, "For in Him dwelleth all the fullness of the Godhead bodily. And ye are complete in Him, which is the head of all principality and power." "If ye then be risen with Christ, seek those things which are above, where Christ sitteth on the right hand of God. Set your affection on things above, not on things on the earth."

This epistle may be outlined as follows:

I. The Exalted Position of Christ (Chapters 1-2) The Doctrinal Section
II. The Expected Practice of the Believer (Chapters 3-6) The Practice Section

I Thessalonians

I Thessalonians is an exemplary epistle of Paul. In this epistle, Paul expresses his joy for the growth of the believers since they received the gospel. Thessalonica was a prominent seaport and capital of the Roman province of Macedonia. Thessalonica had a great population of Jews; however, a great many Gentiles were being attracted to Judaism because of their disdain with Greek paganism.

Paul established the church of Thessalonica during his second missionary journey. This epistle was probably written from Corinth about A.D. 51. With Paul reasoning with the Thessalonians in the synagogue, many of them received the word and thus were saved (Acts 17:1).

In this epistle, Paul is commending this church for the way in which they received the gospel, and the manner by which they expressed the gospel. In essence, Paul is expressing thanksgiving to God because this church had exceptional faith, diligent service and patient steadfastness in view of the persecution they were undergoing. One of Paul's central purposes for writing this epistle was not only to thank God for the expression of the believers' faith, hope and love (Chapter 1), but Paul also had another purpose for writing this book. Paul vigorously defended his motives for his ministry among the believers because his critics claimed that Paul ministered for mercenary gains (Chapter 2).

Paul's purpose for writing this epistle was to exhort and encourage the Thessalonians believers to persevere in light of the trials they were experiencing (Chapter 3). Paul endeavored to correct a misunderstanding the believers had regarding the relationship of the dead in Christ to the Lord's coming; thus, Paul comforted the believers with the assurance that the "dead in Christ" believers, as well as the "believers alive at His coming," will all experience the bliss of the rapture (Chapter 4).

Lastly, Paul's purpose for writing this epistle was to instruct the Thessalonians regarding their spiritual leader's conduct and worship (Chapter 5). This epistle may be outlined as follows:

I.   Paul's Experience with the Thessalonians Believers (Chapters 1-3) Personal
II. Paul's Exhortation to the Thessalonians Believers (Chapters 4-5) Practical

II Thessalonians

The sequel to I Thessalonians is II Thessalonians which was written by the Apostle Paul from Corinth in A.D. 51. Paul wrote this epistle to comfort and correct a severe problem that had upset the spiritual health of the church. The problem that prompted Paul to write this epistle was the erroneous teaching of the false teachers, with their claim that the "Day of the Lord" had already arrived.

With such a hideous claim, the false teachers had greatly upset the minds and hearts of the saints, because in the minds and hearts of the saints, they concluded that they had missed the "Day of Christ." Because of the persecution in which they were experiencing, they were thinking that the "Day of the Lord" had overtaken them.

The "Day of the Lord" is a period of time that begins with the tribulation period and goes throughout the Millennium. It is a period that includes both blessings and cursings. Such a claim by these false teachers greatly disturbed the hearts and minds of the Thessalonian saints.

While Paul was with this growing church, he taught with diligence the "imminent return of Christ." He taught that the Lord could come and dispatch His church at any moment. The next event on God's eschatological calendar is the "Rapture of the Church."

By the term eschatology, the reference is to the end-time events. In following God's time table for events correctly, the Rapture will come first, followed by the Day of the Lord. But the false teachers had the saints disturbed in thinking that because of their experience in persecution that they were in the midst of the "Day of the Lord."

To combat the false teachers' claim, Paul will comfort and also instruct the saints that certain things must take place before that period – spiritual rebellion or apostasy must take place and the revelation of the man of lawlessness, the Antichrist, must make his arrival when the restrainer, The Holy Spirit, is removed (II Thessalonians 2:6-9).

Paul's only prescription to the hideous teaching of the false teachers is a high dosage of God's word. The abounding theme for this book is the coming of the Lord. The Lord's coming back is a most comforting promise to any saint. When the Lord comes the second time, He will pick up His church – a group of called believers since Acts Chapter 2. At the Rapture, only the saints of this church age will meet Him in the mid-air (I Thessalonians 4:13-18, I Corinthians 15:51-58).

After the church goes to heaven with the bridegroom, The Lord Jesus, then the tribulation period will begin. The Day of the Lord begins the Tribulation Period. Every saint of this church age who has placed their faith in Christ's finished work on Calvary is exempted from the wrath (Tribulation Period) to come (I Thessalonians 1:10, 5:9).

The church will be raptured before that awful seven years of tribulation. Certainly, this epistle is an awesome one instructing us that we have been exempted from that awful event – the tribulation period. The troubles experienced in this present age are no comparison to the awful event of the tribulation period. To read about this awful period, the curious mind should read Revelation 6-18. II Thessalonians can be outlined as follows:

I. Paul's Commendation and Encouragement in View of Their Persecution – II Thessalonians 1:1-12
II. Paul's Explanation Concerning the Day of the Lord – II Thessalonians 2:1-17

III. Paul's Admonition to the Church – II Thessalonians 3:1-10

Lastly, the key verse of this epistle is found in II Thessalonians 2:2-3, which says, "That ye be not soon shaken in mind, or be troubled, neither by spirit, nor by word, nor by letter as from us, as that the Day of Christ (Day of the Lord) is at hand." "Let no man deceive you by any means: for that day shall come, except there come a falling away first, and that man of sin be revealed, the son of perdition."

I Timothy

I & II Timothy and Titus are called the "Pastoral Epistles."

Paul writes this Pastoral Epistle from Macedonia in about A.D. 62-63. The aged Apostle Paul is writing this epistle to Timothy, his son in the ministry. Timothy was the son of a Greek Gentile father and a religious mother named Eunice (II Timothy 1:5, Acts 16:1-3). Timothy, the recipient of godly teachings, was no doubt converted under Paul's teachings, and became intimately associated with Paul during his second missionary journey.

In this pastoral letter, Paul is exhorting Timothy to remain steadfast in delivering the word of God, in view of the prevalence of false teachings in the Ephesus church. Moreover, Timothy must make every diligent effort to maintain public worship and to develop solid leaders in the churches in Ephesus.

With reference to the prevalence of false teachings in our contemporary setting, we need to develop leaders to combat the errors being advanced today. We need leaders who will be diligent in proclaiming what "thus says the Lord." It is the task of spiritual leaders to maintain the purity of the faith by committing those truths to able men, for Paul said in II Timothy 2:2 – "And the things that thou has heard of me among many witnesses, the same commit thou to faithful men, who shall be able to teach others also."

By following the directives of this verse, leaders will be passing on the torch of good teachings to other generations, thus the purity of the faith will be preserved. Spiritual leaders should continue to stand firm in the basic beliefs of the faith, such as: the Inspiration of the scriptures, Virgin Birth of Christ, the Incarnation of Christ, the Substitutionary Atonement of Christ, the Resurrection of Christ, His Ascension and even His Second Coming.

Also in this church manual, Paul will exhort Timothy to live exemplary before the church so that his youthfulness might not be a hindrance to the gospel but an aid to it (I Timothy 4:12). Some of the other pertinent and important subjects that Paul covers are: the law (1:7-11), prayer (2:1-8), the attire and appearance of women (2:9-15), the qualifications of bishops or elders and deacons (3:1-13), the last days (4:1-3), care of widows (5:3-16), and the use of money (6:6-19). This Pastoral Epistle may be outlined this way:

I. Introduction Chapter 1:1-2
II. Paul's Exhortation Regarding Doctrine Chapter 1:3-20
III. Paul's Exhortation Regarding Public Worship Chapter 2:1-15
IV. Paul's Exhortation Regarding Leaders Chapter 3:1-16
V. Paul's Exhortation Regarding Dangers Chapter 4:1-16
VI. Paul's Exhortation Regarding Different Duties to be Performed Chapters 5:1-6:21

II Timothy

II Timothy is one of the "Pastoral Epistles." Paul is writing this book from a Roman prison. Facing the prospect of being martyred for his faith in Jesus Christ, Paul exudes a confident assurance. One of the great statements that he made is found in the latter part of II Timothy 1:12 when he said, "for I know whom I have believed, and am persuaded that He is able to keep that which I have committed unto Him against that day."

Instead of Paul allowing his circumstance to cause him to be bitter, it made him better! In that Roman prison cell, Paul is writing to his son in the ministry, alerting him to the challenges of the ministry, imparting to him the wisdom and the encouragement needed in view of the fact of the oppositions and hardships that Timothy will face as he ministers in Ephesus.

Paul stresses the significance to Timothy of living a godly life among the people, so that his ministry might be an asset, and not a liability. Paul exhorts Timothy "to preach the word in season and out of season" (II Timothy 4:2).

Timothy was to remain steadfast in dispensing God's truth even when people "will not endure sound doctrine" (v.3). Timothy was well trained in the scriptures, having been taught by his mother Eunice and his grandmother, Lois, and further schooled by the Apostle himself.

Now Timothy must use his spiritual arsenal to counteract the prevalence of false teachings. The theme of this pastoral manual is Paul's exhortation to Timothy to remain strong and to be encouraged as he faces the assaults of the enemies to the Gospel of Jesus Christ.

Some of the key verses of this pastoral manual are found in II Timothy 2:3-4 and II Timothy 3:14-17, which read, "You therefore must endure hardship as a good soldier of Jesus Christ. No one engaged in warfare entangles himself with the affairs of this life, that he may please Him who enlisted him as a soldier" (2:3-4). "But as for you, continue in the things which you have learned and have been assured of, knowing from whom you have learned them, and that from childhood you have known the Holy Scriptures, which are about to make you wise for salvation through faith which is in Christ Jesus.

All Scriptures is given by inspiration of God, and is profitable for doctrine, for reproof, for correction, for instruction in righteousness, that the man of God may be complete, thoroughly equipped for every good work" (3:14-17).

II Timothy may be outlined as follows:

I. Words of Gratitude for Timothy Chapter 1:1-7
II. The Summons given to Timothy Chapter 1:8-18
III. The Nature of a Good Minister Chapter 2:1-26
IV. The Danger of Apostasy given to Timothy Chapter 3:1-17
V. The Responsibility to Preach given to Timothy
    Chapter 4:1-5
VI. Concluding Words regarding Paul's Fate Chapter 4:6-22

Titus

Located on the Mediterranean Island was a place called Crete; its inhabitants had a bad reputation for being immoral, abounding in wicked activities. To be called a "Cretan" was similar to being called "vile" and "wicked."

Paul had visited Crete following his Roman imprisonment but dispatched Titus with the challenging task of appointing elders and to give oversight for the churches in Crete. Thus, Paul will advise Titus to appoint elders so that the churches will be properly organized and managed. More importantly, Paul will stress to Titus that each age group mentioned in Chapter 2 (aged men and women, young men and women, and servants) must exhibit the proper character and conduct that is consistent with the profession of their claimed faith in God.

In addition to Titus' responsibility to properly organize the churches, there was also a grave need that he refute the false teachers in Crete, who were guilty of distorting the truth of the gospel (1:10-16). These false teachers were guilty of subverting sound doctrine.

The theme of this epistle is Paul's exhortation to Titus to appoint elders in the church for organization and that each member would live out the truth of the gospel through godly living. Some of the key verses of this epistle are found in Titus 1:5 and 3:8, and they read, "For this reason (cause) left I thee in Crete, that thou shouldest set in order the things that are wanting, and ordain elders in every city, as I had appointed thee"; "This is a faithful saying, and these things I will that thou affirm constantly, that they which have believed in God might be careful to maintain good works. These things are good and profitable unto men."

This epistle has a brief outline.

I. Select Proven Leaders (Chapter 1)
II. Proclaim Sound Doctrine (Chapter 2)
III. Practice Good Works (Chapter 3)

Christian theology references found in the book of Titus are: 1:1-4; 2:11-14; 3:4-7.

Philemon

The book of Philemon, exudes tenderness and warmth in dealing with a delicate and difficult problem regarding a slave owner, Philemon, and his slave, Onesimus. In this letter, Paul will address in a tactful way the Christian approach needed in dealing with the issue when a party has been wronged, and the proper forgiveness and restoration that should be granted – especially when both parties are "brethren in Christ."

Apparently, Onesimus had wronged his slave owner, Philemon, and had taken flight to the imperial city of Rome, where he comes in contact with Paul who was incarcerated (Acts 28:30-31). While in Rome, Paul shares the gospel of the grace of God with Onesimus and Onesimus is now saved. Now that Onesimus is saved, Paul knows that Onesimus has a Christian responsibility to return to Philemon – but the question that should be raised is, "How should Onesimus be received?"

In the highest art of diplomacy and Christian tact, Paul will beseech Philemon, asking of a favor because of their mutual relationship to Christ and to each other. Paul was well aware of the offense that Onesimus had committed, and the punishment that Onesimus should receive; however, on the basis of Christian love and forgiveness, Paul is appealing to Philemon that he would receive Onesimus in a new light, "Not now as a servant, but above a servant, a brother beloved..."(v. 16).

Within the framework of Christianity, this book informs us that any situation can be resolved where there has been a breach in a relationship. Christians will have situations wherein a certain party is wronged, but as Christians, the bible has given to us the mandate to forgive (Matthew 18:21-22).

In this delicate situation, Paul will appeal for Onesimus' forgiveness and restoration – and within the frame work of Christianity, Paul will illustrate the basis of his appeal by offering to pay any debt which stands due to Philemon (v. 18). This verse is the highlight of the epistle, for it says, "If he hath wronged thee, or oweth thee ought, put that on mine account."

Through Paul's act, a portrayal of what Christ did for the believers is seen. Paul was willing to serve as a substitute for Onesimus – willing to pay in full the debt to which Onesimus had incurred. That is what Christ did for us, having paid in full, the debt of sin which we received from our forefather, Adam (Romans 5:12; II Corinthians 5:21).

The outline of this book is:

I. A Prayer of Gratitude for Philemon (vv. 1-7).
II. A Plea of Paul for Onesimus (vv. 8-16).
III. A Guarantee of Paul to Philemon (vv. 17-25).

Hebrews

The author of the epistle of Hebrews is questionable; however, despite the uncertainty of its author, the richness of this book's message remains unmarred. The epistle presents a presentation of the grandeur of the person of Christ, showing that Jesus Christ is superior to anything that Judaism has to offer.

The Hebrew Christians in this epistle were under severe persecution since embracing Christ. Because of their persecution as a result of their faith in Christ, they felt pressure to revert to their former religion of Judaism and abandon Christianity. But the author of this epistle wrote to persuade these believers that to abandon Christianity for Judaism would be like forsaking "substance for shadow" or the "antitype for the type."

Why would they want to abandon Christianity – for Christ, the Head of the Christian movement, is exceedingly better than Judaism with its rituals and ceremonies. In spite of the Hebrew Christians' persecution, the writer will exhort them to "press on unto perfection" (Hebrews 6:1).

The author exhorts his readers to a life of faith by, first of all, presenting the person Christ, showing that the person of Christ is superior to the prophets (Hebrews 1:1-3); He is superior to the angels (Hebrews 1:4 – 2:18); He is superior to Moses (Hebrews 3:1 – 4:13); He is superior to the Aaronic

Priesthood (Hebrews 4:14-7:28); Christ's Covenant is superior to the Old Covenant (Hebrews 8:1-13); and Christ has a superior sanctuary and sacrifice (Hebrews 9:1-10:18).

After presenting the person of Christ, the author will exhort his readers to an exemplary walk of faith by challenging them to look at those who triumph in faith despite the many odds in which they faced" (Hebrews 11). Despite the many trials of their faith, these Old Testament worthies placed their faith in God, trusting solely in God's promises even before the proofs of His promises were realized demonstrating exceptional faith indeed.

Christians can triumph in faith as we look "unto Jesus, the author and finisher of our faith" (Hebrews 12:2). As the author and finisher of our faith, Jesus Christ endured hostility, resulting in His death and resurrection for us. And as Jesus endured Divine discipline, Christians too must endure Divine chastisement, which is a proof that we belong to Him (Hebrews 12:1-19).

Lastly, the author exhorted his readers to a life of loving concern for one another (Chapter 13), concluding with a masterful benediction (v. 20-21), as he gives his closing remarks. There are several warning passages (Hebrews 2:1-4, 3:7-4:13, 5:11-6:20, 10:19-39, 12:25-29) interspersed in the author's presentation to caution his Jewish audience in recognizing the severity of their pressured position to abandon Christianity for Judaism.

This book is outlined this way:

I. The Supreme Presentation of the Person and Work of Christ (Hebrews 1:1-10:39)
II. The Supreme Example of the Life of Faith (Hebrews 11:1-13:25)

James

This epistle was written by our Lord's half-brother James (Matthew 13:55-56). James, who did not become a believer until after Christ's resurrection, was one of the pillars of the church (St. John 7:5, Acts 1:14, I Corinthians 15:7), Galatians 2:9, Acts 15:13-19). The book of James is a down-to-earth epistle dealing with the subject of "faith." But the book of James is concerned with a faith that works; a faith that bears fruit; a faith that is productive.

The book of James states that the man who verbalizes his faith must support it by his works; otherwise, if his faith is not backed up by his deeds, his faith is dead indeed. James is advocating that the genuineness of a man's faith will really be measured by the quality of his good deeds. In this epistle, James is advancing that the genuineness of a man's faith produces a vital change in a man's personal conduct and character. The productivity of a man's faith is seen in his ability to withstand the trials of life, knowing that trials are permitted by God to enhance spiritual maturity (James 1:1-12).

Although a believer may experience trials (testing) – v. 12, no believer can say that he or she was tempted by God, for God does not solicit any believer to evil, (v. 13-15), but are drawn by his own lust. In chapter two, James further shows that a working faith will not be partial to others (Chapter 2:1-3), especially in treating the poor unjustly (Chapter 2:4-13).

One of the key verses of this book that brings out James' argument that "genuine faith produces works" is found in James 2:14 which says, "What doth it profit, my brethren, though a man say he hath faith, and have not works? Can faith save him?"

From this verse many writers have concluded that the Apostle Paul, and the Lord's half-brother, James, were at odds with one another on the subject of "how a man can be justified (declared righteous). But in Romans Chapter 4, Paul is advocating that a man is justified before God by his faith; whereas, James is advancing that the evidence of a man's justification is demonstrated by his good works before men. Good works will not save us; but our good works are evidence of our salvation.

Salvation is always by grace through faith (Ephesians 2:8); however, good works are evidence of being saved. Another facet of truth that shows that genuine faith should be productive is seen in the control of the tongue (Chapter 3). Real and living faith will be seen by controlling that small member of our bodies, the tongue.

Lastly, in Chapters 4 and 5 James shows that a faith that works will be victorious over worldliness and will patiently withstand the sufferings of this present life in the light of the glorious coming of the Lord (James 5:7-12). The outline of this book may be observed as follows:

I. The Trials of Faith, James 1:1-18
II. The True Nature of Faith, James 1:19-5:6
III. The Testimony of Faith, James 5:7-20

I Peter

Peter is writing to Jewish believers who are being persecuted. In fact, these saints were dispersed because of their persecution and Peter reminds them that they need to respond to their struggle in a godly manner, knowing that they have been born again to a lively hope.

In any conflict of this life, the Christian needs to know that he can endure because of his perfect standing in Christ; conflicts can never alter son-ship; it may affect our fellowship when we are not trusting in the sufficiency of God. In the midst of the trials of this life, Christians should conduct themselves courageously for the person and program of Christ.

Christians should not be shocked at any ordeal of this life, because as Christians, we are instructed that suffering is our lot (II Timothy 3:12), for in following Christ, He also suffered and died (I Peter 2:21; 3:18; 4:1, 12-14).

The theme of this epistle is "The Christian's Appropriate Response to Suffering." One of the key verses of the epistle of Peter is found in I Peter 4:12-13, and it says, "Beloved, think it not strange concerning the fiery trial which is to try you, as though some strange thing happened unto you: But rejoice, inasmuch as ye are partakers of Christ's sufferings; that, when His glory shall be revealed, ye may be glad also with exceeding joy."

The outline of I Peter is as follows:

I. The Security of the Believer (I Peter 1:1-2:12)
II. The Submission of the Believer (I Peter 2:13-3:12)
III. The Suffering of the Believer (I Peter 3:13-5:14)

II Peter

Whereas, I Peter dealt with problems lingering from the outside (persecution), II Peter is dealing with defection or false teaching from the inside. The heretical teachers of Peter's time had invaded the church with their damaging doctrine, seeking to undermine the faith of the believers. To counteract their heretical doctrine and the lifestyle that they propagated, Peter exhorted his audience of their need to "grow in grace, and in the knowledge of our Lord and Saviour Jesus Christ," (II Peter 3:18) and to embrace a lifestyle of godliness in view of the coming of the Lord Jesus Christ.

The destructive teachers of Peter's day were seeking to seduce believers into error and immorality. Bad doctrine will produce immoral living. To counteract any heretical teachings, there is a grave need to know the truth. The best way to "detect counterfeit currency is to know your currency well."

Not only did Peter remind his audience that false teachers had invaded their rank with their false doctrine, but he also reminded them that God will certainly judge them; in fact, they will not escape God's judgment just like the fallen angels and the cities of Sodom and Gomorrah of the Old Testament didn't escape.

In this epistle, Peter talks about the scoffers who refuted the doctrine of the Second Coming of Christ, insisting that from the beginning nothing really catastrophic had happened. However, to refute their claim, Peter shows three catastrophic events that have and will happen: creation, the flood and in the future, the dissolution of the present heaven and earth. The promise of God's return will be fulfilled, and the two reasons for His delay are found in verses 8 and 9, and they read: "But beloved, be not ignorant of this one thing, that one day is with the Lord as a thousand years, and a thousand years as one day. The Lord is not slack concerning His promise, as some men count slackness; but is longsuffering to us-ward, not willing that any should perish, but that all should come to repentance."

What are the two reasons for God's delay? The first reason is that God does not perceive time as man (v. 8); and the second reason is that God desires that more individuals repent (v. 9). As Peter closes this epistle, having discussed the certainty of the Lord's coming, he exhorts these believers to live lives of holiness, steadfastness and growth (II Peter 3:14-18). The outline of this book is as follows:

I. The Development of Christian Character II Peter 1:1-21
II. The Damaging Heresy of False Teachers II Peter 2:1-22
III. The Dynamic Surety of Christ's Return II Peter 3:1-8

I John

In this epistle of love, John is writing with a desire that every child of God experiences the delight of having fellowship with God. This epistle was written by John, the apostle, in Ephesus around A.D. 90. The basic theme of this I John is fellowship with God.

In this epistle, John, the apostle, gives three tests for knowing that a child of God is in fellowship with God: confession of sins (I John 1:9); walking in the truth (I John 2:4-5); and loving the brethren (I John 2:9-10). Moreover, the apostle John gives unto us three lofty concepts about the character of God: God is light (I John 1:5); God is love (I John 4:8, 16); and God is life (I John 5:11).

With those three concepts in mind, it is virtually impossible to have fellowship with God if one is walking in darkness. Therefore, every child of God should "walk in the light, as He is in the light" to maintain fellowship with God and with one another (I John 1:7).

And how can one "walk in the light?' We "walk in the light" by confessing regularly our sins (I John 1:9), and by keeping Christ's commandments (2:4-5), and by loving one another (2:9-10). The word "love" is used often in this epistle, not as a nebulous or vague concept, but as an expression of God's unconditional love for us; thus, it is a love that gives, and not receives. This love is demonstrated on Calvary, when Christ gave Himself as a substitute for our sins. Through our acceptance of His finished work on Calvary, fellowship with God was made possible.

In this epistle, the apostle John is refuting a heresy called Gnosticism. The Gnostics advanced that matter was inherently evil, and therefore, a Divine being could not take on human flesh. Thus, the Gnostics denied the incarnation of Christ.

This doctrine is dangerous – to deny the Son is to deny the Father (I John 2:23). To become a member of the family of God, you must believe in God's only provision for sin, Jesus Christ. Jesus Christ is the only way to the Father, for Jesus says in St. John 14:6, that, "I am the way, the truth, and the life: no man cometh unto the Father, but by me."

The epistle of I John is outlined as follows:

I. The Essence of Fellowship (I John 1:1-2:27)
II. The Evidence of Fellowship (I John 2:28-5:21).

II John

The author of II John is the Apostle John, the Apostle of love. This brief letter – the second shortest, III John is a little shorter than II John – was written by the Apostle John around A.D. 90, probably in Ephesus. II John is a concise letter written to a chosen lady and her children who were undergoing or experiencing the threat of following false teachers.

In this letter, John exhorts his audience not to embrace those who seek to decimate the truth. The theme of this letter is to remain steadfast in the practice and purity of the apostolic doctrine that John's readers had "heard from the beginning" (v. 6).

The Apostle delivers a severe warning in an effort to attack this hideous problem which is found in verse 10, and that verse says, "If there come any unto you, and bring not this doctrine, receive him not in your house, neither bid him God speed."

In John's day, there were false teachers who denied the incarnation of Jesus Christ. To deny the doctrine of the incarnation is to distort the central teaching of Christianity. To deny the central truth regarding Christ's incarnation, is to deny His humanity, His death and resurrection, and even His coming back again. To deny the doctrine of His incarnation is damaging to our faith, indeed.

Even though John commends these saints for "walking in the truth (v. 4); he also will exhort these saints to embrace love, one for another; however, in exercising their love, they must exhibit a love that is discerning, in view of the fact, that they must not show hospitality to false teachers who seek to destroy the central teaching of Christianity. We are to manifest love to everyone – but it must be love based on truth – not love that is merely sentimental without any regard to truth.

The key verses of this letter are verses 10 and 11. John is saying in these verses that these deceivers (false teachers) must be avoided; thus, don't support their ministry nor give them an encouraging greeting. The best way to withstand false teachers - is to "walk in the truth" (v. 4), and walk in love (vs. 5-6). And when we are practicing these two exhortations, we will not embrace the teaching of false teachers (vs. 7-11).

This letter is outlined as follows:

I. Remain in God's Commandments (vs. 1-6)
II. Reject the Teaching of False Teachers (vs. 7-13)

III John

The letter of III John was written by the Apostle John around A.D. 90. In all three letters (I John, II John, III John) there has been an emphasis placed on the word "fellowship." In I John, the Apostle writes about fellowship with God; in II John, he exhorts the believers to avoid fellowship with false teachers; in III John, he promotes fellowship with Christian brothers.

The main recipient of this letter was Gaius, a good Christian example. He is commended by the Apostle John for his exemplary behavior in persistently "walking in the truth" (v. 3). Such a walk is not only pleasing to the Lord, but it serves as a powerful witness to those around you. Walking in the truth conveys the idea of ordering one's life by the word of God. Such a walk is needed in a world tainted by the darkness of sin and corruption. Saints who are walking according to God's word are letting their light shine in the midst of a decadent society (Matthew 5:16; Philippians 2:15).

In contrast to the godly behavior of Gaius, Diotrephes was a man who was arrogant and wanted to display his preeminence in the church. He defied the authority of the Apostle John. Whereas, Gaius was loyal to the word by displaying hospitality to the messengers of the gospel, even to the point of being generous toward them (v. 5-6); however, Diotrephes, the arrogant one, did not receive the messengers of the gospel (v. 9).

Diotrephes' behavior caused John to use words, not of commendation, but of condemnation (v. 10). Another exemplary Christian praised by the Apostle John was Demetrius (v. 12). The letter closes with John's hope of a close visit with them (v. 13-14).

This letter is outlined as follows:

I. Walking in the Truth (v. 1-8) (Gaius' Character and Good Conduct)
II. Walking in Error (v. 9-14) (Diotrephes' Arrogance and Evil Conduct)

Jude

The writer of this epistle is Jude, the brother of our Lord Jesus Christ (Matthew 13:55). He, along with his brother, James, the writer of the epistle of James, became a believer after the resurrection of Jesus (St. John 7:1-9; Acts 1:14). This epistle was probably written in A.D. 66-80, with the place of writing being unknown.

Jude's original intent was to write to his readers regarding their common salvation; however, because of the urgent danger to his readers, he directed his attention instead to those who were guilty of trying to destroy the gospel through the propagation of false teaching. The prevalence of false teaching was a threat in Jude's day, and it remains a menace today.

In this epistle, Jude recalls that the threat of false doctrine and rebellion are not subjects with which God hasn't dealt. Because of the onslaughts of false doctrine and rebellion, God has in the past judged the following: disobedient Israel, fallen angels, Sodom and Gomorrah, Cain, Balaam and Korah. Because of the urgent threat of apostasy and false teaching, Jude sensed the urgent need to challenge his readers to "contend earnestly for the faith (v. 3).

Believers today are to be ardent defenders of the faith – not in any way compromising the truth of the word, as found in verse 4, "For false teachers have crept into the church unnoticed, turning the grace of God into lasciviousness" – granting or permitting people a license to do as they please.

The general theme of this epistle is Jude's concern with the false teaching of these heretics in the church and the believer's appropriate response to their dangerous teaching. The key verse of this magnificent epistle is found in verse 3, for it reads – "Beloved, when I gave all diligence to write unto you of the common salvation, it was needful for me to write unto you, and exhort you that ye should earnestly contend for the faith which was once delivered unto the saints."

The outline of Jude is as follows:

I. The Prevalence of False Teachers v. 1-4.
II. The Prevailing Problem of False Teachers, and God's Past Judgment of Rebellion v. 5-16.
III. A Pressing Defense Against False Teachers v. 17-25

Revelation

Whereas the book of Genesis speaks of beginnings, the book of Revelation speaks of completion, or the consummation of things. In this prophetic work, given to the Apostle John in a vision of the risen Christ, God's scheme of redemption is brought to completion, and His awesome name, which is Holy, is vindicated before creation.

The book of Revelation focuses on prophetic events – events that will surely transpire. The title of the book means the "unveiling" or "disclosure". Thus, this book unveils the character and program of God.

This book was written by the Apostle John, the son of Zebedee (Revelation 1:1). The Apostle John, banished to the island of Patmos because of his testimony of Christ, probably wrote this book during the severe reign of Domitian, an emperor of Rome, around A.D. 81-96.

The central figure of the book is the risen and exalted Christ. In chapter 1, in His exalted glory, Christ is directing the churches of Asia Minor, with each church receiving a message (chapters 2-3). In chapters 4-5, the exalted Lamb is worshiped, for He along is worthy of praise and honor because of the great redemption He wrought (Revelation 5:9-10).

After the Apostle John's heavenly scene of the Risen Christ, the seven year period of tribulation on this earth is mentioned in which the wrath of the exalted Lamb is unleashed (chapters 6-18), culminating with the coming of the Lamb to the earth as He vindicates His righteousness (chapter 19), and establishes His millennial reign (chapter 20).

Satan and his cohorts will be consigned eventually to the lake of fire (chapter 20:10); and after the unsaved of all ages are sentenced at the Great White Throne (chapter 20:11-15), the Apostle John writes about the coming of the new heavens and the new earth (chapters 21-22) after the desolation of the old heaven and earth (II Peter 3:12-13).

From chapter 1:19, the book of Revelation may be outlined as follows:

I. The Things Which Thou Hast Seen (Chapter 1)
II. The Things Which Are (Chapters 2-3)
III. The Things Which Shall Be Here After (Chapters 4-22)

BIBLIOGRAPHY

Geisler, Norman L. A Popular Survey of the Old Testament. Grand Rapids: Baker Book House, 1977.

Hester, H. I. The Heart of the New Testament. Liberty, Missouri: The Quality Press, Inc., 1963.

Jensen, Irving L. Jensen's Survey of the Old Testament. Chicago: Moody Press, 1960.

Jensen, Irving L. Jensen's Survey of the New Testament. Chicago: Moody Press, 1960.

Mears, Henrietta C. What the Bible is All About. Glendale, California, USA: A Division of G/L Publications, 1953.

Unger, Merrill F. Unger's Bible Handbook. Chicago: Moody Press, 1966.

Walvoord, John F. and Zuck, Roy B. The Bible Knowledge Commentary Old Testament. Colorado Springs, Colorado: David C. Cook, 1983.

Walvoord, John F. and Zuck, Roy B. The Bible Knowledge Commentary New Testament. Colorado Springs, Colorado: David C. Cook, 1983.

Wilkinson, Bruce and Boa, Kenneth. Talk Thru the Bible. Nashville, Tennessee: Thomas Nelson Publishers, 1983.

Wood, Leon. A Survey of Israel's History. Grand Rapids, Michigan: Zondervan Publishing House, 1970.

About the Author:
PASTOR JOHNNY CALVIN SMITH

"Being confident of this very thing, that he which hath begun a good work in you will perform it until the day of Jesus Christ." Philippians 1:6

The Reverend Johnny Calvin Smith has a powerful message for all mankind. This man of God speaks without reservation, proclaiming the gospel of grace, calling for repentance, faith, and hope in our Lord Jesus Christ. Rev. Smith is in his sixth year as Pastor of the Mount Moriah Missionary Baptist Church, Dallas, Texas.

He received his formal education in the Dallas Public School system, earning his diploma from L.G. Pinkston High School in 1970. He furthered his education by earning the following degrees and certifications:

Educational Background
Undergraduate
Jarvis Christian College,
August 1970 – May 1972
Southern Methodist University,
August 1972-May 1974
Bachelor of Business Administration Degree

Biblical Studies
Southern Bible Institute,
August 1975 – May 1980
Diploma in Preliminary Bible Program;
Bachelor of Arts in Biblical Studies
Dallas Bible College
August 1982 – May 1984

Graduate Studies
Dallas Theological Seminary,
August 1984 – May 1991
Master of Arts in Biblical Studies

"I charge thee therefore before God, and the Lord Jesus Christ...Preach the word..." II Timothy 4:1-2.

Ordained as a Minister at Mount Moriah Missionary Baptist Church in 1977, he began in 1982 serving as Director of the Board of Christian Education until accepting the pastorate in 2007. Additionally, he has served as a Sunday School Teacher, Instructor of Evangelical Training Association; and Mount Moriah Disciple Institute. He has also served as a part-time Instructor at Southern Bible Institute since 1985. He rightly divides the Word in his inspirational column, "Devotional Thought From The Word" published in The Dallas Post Tribune.

Pastor Smith and his wife, Violet, have been married for 38 years and are the proud of parents of one daughter, Joy (Brad) McBeth and two sons Rev. Jonathan (Christina) Smith and Jared Smith. They have been blessed with five grandchildren, Josiah, Jeremiah, Jillian, Jessica and Jackson.

Pastor Smith has a great love and devotion for his family and a sincere passion and concern for the youth of today. As a retired Mathematics/Science Teacher in the Dallas Public Schools, Pastor Smith expresses "I am praying that youth of today will remain steadfast in their walk with the Lord and avoid the pitfalls of seemingly worldly pleasures presented by Satan."

The Johnny Calvin Smith Family

Also from Searchlight Press

Developing Oneness in Marriage:
A 'How-to' for Husbands
by Rev. Dr. Lloyd C. Blue
(Searchlight Press, 2011)

Character Is Key:
In Sports and in Life
by Eddie Hill and Dr. Jim Moore
(Searchlight Press, 2010)

Headed the Wrong Direction?
Calling Us and Others
Back from the Edge
by Rev. Wade J. Simmons
(Searchlight Press, 2011)

Wonderworking Power:
A Fresh Translation
of the Gospel of Mark
by John Cunyus
(Searchlight Press, 2011)

A Survery of the Scriptures, 218

Searchlight Press
Who are you looking for?
Publishers of thoughtful Christian books since 1994.
5634 Ledgestone Drive
Dallas, TX 75214-2026
214.662.5494
info@Searchlight-Press.com
www.Searchlight-Press.com